ARCHAEOLOGICAL EXCAVATIONS AT AZ I:10:30 (ASM), A SINAGUA SETTLEMENT: TOWNSEND-DIVIDE UNIT I, U.S. HIGHWAY 89, COCONINO COUNTY, ARIZONA

by

Martyn D. Tagg and Robert W. Layhe

Contributions by

Anne R. Baldwin
J. Michael Bremer
Lisa W. Huckell
Barbara A. Murphy
Marilyn B. Saul
Arthur W. Vokes
L. Keiko Yoshikawa

Cultural Resource Management Division
Arizona State Museum
University of Arizona

Archaeological Series No. 169

ARCHAEOLOGICAL EXCAVATIONS AT AZ I:10:30 (ASM), A SINAGUA SETTLEMENT: TOWNSEND-DIVIDE UNIT I, U.S. HIGHWAY 89, COCONINO COUNTY, ARIZONA

by

Martyn D. Tagg and Robert W. Layhe

Contributions by

Anne R. Baldwin
J. Michael Bremer
Lisa W. Huckell
Barbara A. Murphy
Marilyn B. Saul
Arthur W. Vokes
L. Keiko Yoshikawa

Prepared for

Arizona Department of Transportation
Project No. F-037-1 (8)

Submitted by

Cultural Resource Management Division
Arizona State Museum
University of Arizona

1985

Archaeological Series No. 169

CONTENTS

FIGURES

TABLES

ACKNOWLEDGMENTS

Even small projects such as the one reported on here necessitate the cooperation and expertise of many individuals. I would like to take this opportunity to express my thanks to those persons whose input enabled this project to come to successful fruition. Lynn S. Teague, Head, Cultural Resource Management Divison, and David A. Gregory, Cultural Resource Management Division's principal investigator for Arizona Department of Transportation (ADOT) projects, provided me with the opportunity to do this project. Both Mr. William Hayden, formerly Manager of Environmental Services, and Bettina Rosenberg, Highway Archaeologist with ADOT, provided the sponsor liason that ensured successful completion of the fieldwork and analysis. Mr. Roy Paxton graciously allowed us to conduct our work on his land. Ed Baca of COMSAN provided backhoe services.

Peter J. Pilles, Jr., Coconino National Forest, provided a well-spring of insight regarding the Sinagua; Dr. Donald Weaver, Museum of Northern Arizona, provided unrestricted access to unpublished manuscripts at that institution.

The field crew was comprised of Anne R. Baldwin, Ronald Beckwith, and Martyn Tagg, to whom I offer my sincerest thanks for their participation in conditions that were sometimes less than ideal. William Deaver removed the archaeomagnetic samples and pitched in for the last few days of field work. Barbara A. Murphy ran archaeomagnetic samples, the results of which are provided in Appendix E.

Anne R. Baldwin and J. Michael Bremer analyzed the Alameda Brown Wares and wrote the section that has been incorporated into the chapter on ceramics. I would also like to thank the contributors of the specialized analyses in this report--Lisa W. Huckell, Marilyn Saul, Arthur W. Vokes, and L. Keiko Yoshikawa--for their timely completion. Ronald Beckwith rendered the excellent figures scattered throughout the text; Janelle Weakly prepared all photographic illustrations. Arthur W. Vokes coordinated the initial laboratory processing of all artifactual materials in his usual efficient manner. Bruce B. Huckell and Kenneth Rozen were helpful with the flaked and ground stone analysis. Dr. Alexander J. Lindsay, Jr. and Dr. Robert B. Neily offered invaluable assistance with the analysis of decorated ceramics.

Carol Heathington, Jeanne Witt, and Ben Smith lent their expertise in the formatting, editing, and word processing aspects of this report. I would like to thank my wife Holly Young for her most welcome input through all stages of this project. I would also like to thank Sharon Bartlett, Administrative Assistant (CRMD), and the Museum bookkeeping staff of Diann Blair, Dola Moore, and Martha Barrow for smoothing over all the rough edges on the administrative side of this project. I would also like to thank Lynn Teague, Peter J. Pilles, Jr., John Madsen, and Christian Downum for reading and offerring their constructive comments and criticisms on a draft version of this report. Although not all of their suggestions have been heeded, I am nevertheless grateful for their input. While all the individuals named above contributed in their various ways, any errors or omissions remain the reponsiblity of the authors.

Robert W. Layhe
Project Director

ABSTRACT

This report describes and discusses archaeological data recovery at a Sinagua site (AZ I:10:30, ASM) within an Arizona Department of Transportation (ADOT) right-of-way near Flagstaff, Arizona. A brief discussion of the research potential of the site and of the cultural history and natural setting of the region is provided. This is followed by feature descriptions, artifact analyses and results, and interpretations of the subsistance patterns, chronology, and external relationships of the inhabitants of the site. Specialized analyses are provided in four appendixes at the end of the report.

The investigations at Townsend-Divide (AZ I:10:30, ASM), involving excavations on a small portion of a larger site, revealed two pit houses and four burials associated with the late Rio de Flag, Angell-Winona phases (A.D. 1000 to 1100). This work added useful information to our understanding of the Sinagua in the Flagstaff region in the Preeruptive-Posteruptive period, just after the formation of Sunset Crater in A.D. 1064 to 1066.

Chapter 1

INTRODUCTION

At the request of the Arizona Department of Transportation (ADOT), the Cultural Resource Management Division of the Arizona State Museum, University of Arizona, conducted an archaeological data recovery program to mitigate the adverse effects of the realignment of U. S. Highway 89 on AZ I:10:30 (ASM), hereafter referred to as Townsend-Divide. Townsend-Divide refers to the entire ADOT highway project and was selected as the name for the archaeological site reported on here. Townsend-Divide is a prehistoric Sinagua site located north of the city limits of Flagstaff, Arizona (Fig. 1.1). The highway improvements consist of widening and realigning approximately 11.37 miles of the existing highway from about the northern Flagstaff city limit to just north of the entrance road into Sunset Crater National Monument. This report covers the archaeological mitigation efforts at one site in Unit I, the southernmost 5.8 miles. In Unit II, the northern section, several sites remain that will receive further archaeological study. The highway improvements involve widening the existing two-lane roadway into a 68-foot four-lane roadway with left turn lanes, curbs, gutters, and sidewalks. The realignment of this roadway will significantly straighten the existing curved roadway and will improve visibility and traffic safety.

Previous archaeological testing and intensive surface collection at Townsend-Divide (Sullivan 1980) indicated the presence of one pit house, one possible prepared floor or occupation surface, a burial, and prehistoric trash deposits. The data recovery program was aimed at relocating these prehistoric features as well as ascertaining the presence of additional features.

Research Potential of Townsend-Divide (AZ:I:10:30, ASM)

A general set of research questions guided the archaeological data recovery at Townsend-Divide. These questions are germane to furthering our understanding of the prehistory of the Sinagua and their adaptation to the region around Flagstaff, Arizona.

1. What is the chronological placement of Townsend-Divide within the established Sinagua cultural-historical framework? From what data sets is this derived?

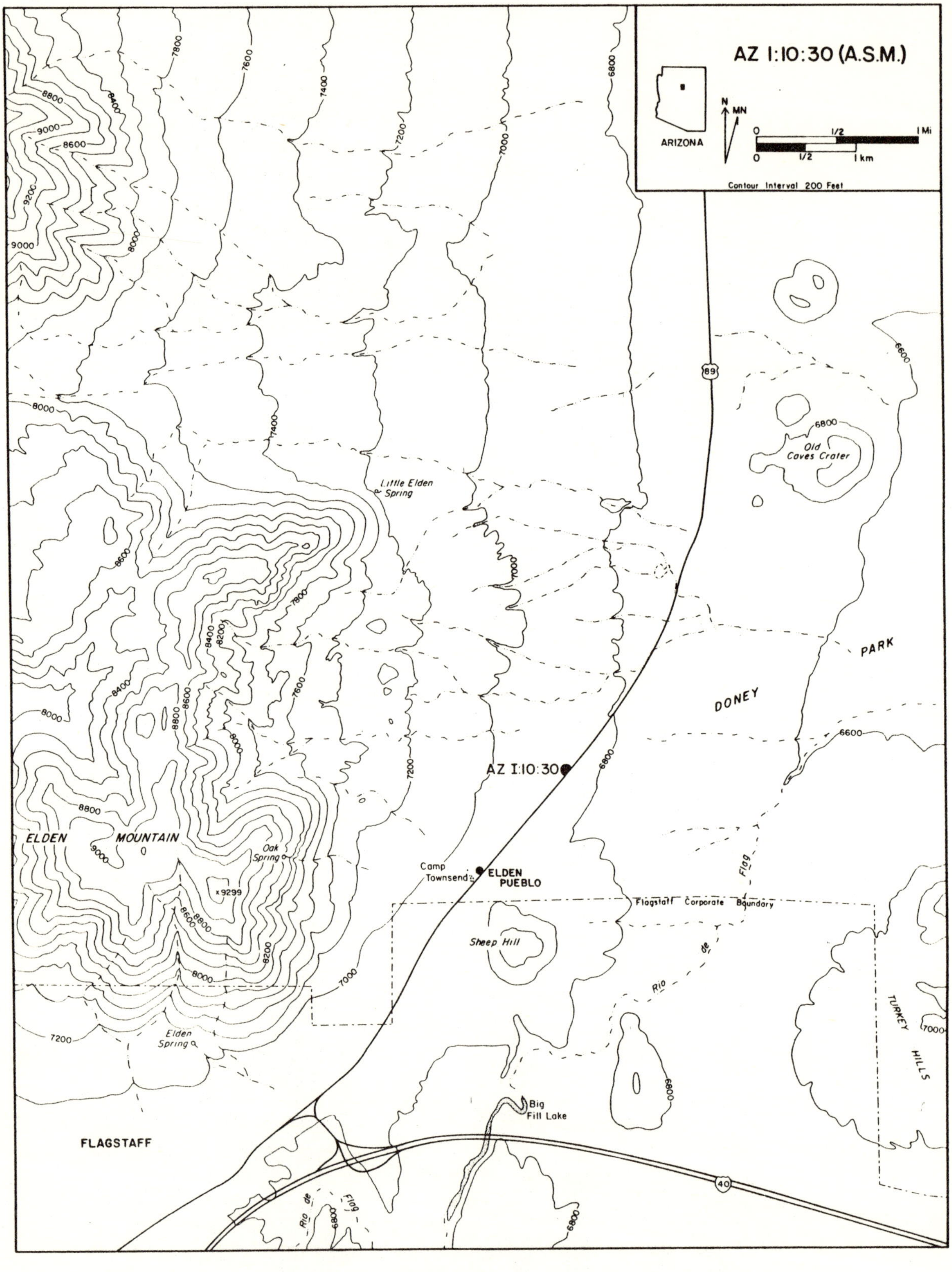

Figure 1.1 Townsend-Divide and vicinity.

2. Is there evidence of occupation at the site prior to, or following, the eruption of Sunset Crater in A.D. 1064 to 1066? Is there occupational continuity spanning both periods?

3. How does Townsend-Divide compare to other known, excavated sites in the area? What subsistence or settlement location evidence is present to verify or repudiate previously established settlement and subsistence models?

4. What evidence is present regarding external contacts either in the form of trade or exchange of goods versus an influx of migrant populations? Is there evidence that the Sinagua may be modeled as middlemen in an exchange or trade network?

5. To what extent does the fact that only a portion of the site is extant affect the inferences derived from the excavated data?

With this broad set of research questions in mind, we may now turn to a discussion of Sinagua culture history and environmental considerations that serve as a background and data base for the current research.

Chapter 2

CULTURAL AND NATURAL SETTING

Culture History and Previous Areal Research Among the Sinagua of Northern Arizona

The Sinagua were a prehistoric cultural group inhabiting the environs in the vicinity of Flagstaff, Arizona (Fig. 1.1). Much of the work on which this section is based derives from Colton's (1939, 1946) seminal work on the Sinagua, McGregor's (1941a) work at Winona, and from more recent investigations by Pilles (1978, 1979).

Sinagua prehistory is generally discussed in two gross time periods with respect to the eruption of Sunset Crater in A.D. 1064 (Pilles 1978, 1979: 461). The Preeruptive period in Sinagua prehistory consists of three separate phases, while the Posteruptive period encompasses four to six phases. These phases will be referred to below in the discussion of both Preeruptive and Posteruptive patterns of Sinagua culture history.

The earliest evidence of the Sinagua as a cultural group is defined as the Cinder Park phase, between A.D. 600 and 700, and is generally contemporaneous with the Basketmaker III period of the Kayenta Anasazi (Colton 1946: 268; Pilles 1978: 128). Pit houses, as might be expected, are the dominant architectural form found during this phase. The pottery is Alameda Brown Ware, characterized by Rio de Flag Brown, and is it constructed by the paddle and anvil technique.

The Cinder Park phase is followed by the Sunset phase, A.D. 700 to 900, and the Rio de Flag phase, A.D. 900 to 1066, corresponding with Pueblo I and early Pueblo II, respectively, of the Kayenta Anasazi. Pilles (1979: 461) notes that during these three phases ". . . ceramics, architectural styles, settlement plans, and subsistence strategies" appear to be rather uniform. This inference is based to date on the fact that so little archaeological work has been conducted at sites of the early phases.

Settlement patterns during the Preeruptive period appears to have been scattered sites of two to five pit houses possibly unified into larger communities (Pilles 1978: 128). The population was centered around the region of Cinder Park and Turkey Tanks, east of Anderson Mesa, and somewhat west of the Mogollon Rim in the Verde Valley (Colton 1946: 247). Madsen (1982, Fig. 2.1) shows population around Sunset Crater, Bonito Park, and Little Elden Mountain during the Preeruptive period. Agriculture was certainly practiced, being concentrated in the fertile parks along the Rio de Flag (Pilles 1978: 129, 1979: 463); it consisted of both dry farming and ak-chin farming.

Some of the later Preeruptive sites may have been the centers of ceremonial activities for a larger community (for example, Breternitz 1959; Wilson 1969) as unusually large pit houses have been interpreted as structures with community functions. Similarly, sites with ball-courts (for example, Camp Ball Court and Doney Park Ball Court) may have functioned as community integrators (Pilles 1978: 129; Fish and others 1980; Madsen 1982: 13). While this is not the place to discuss at great length the concept of the community, recent research by Neily (1983) suggests that the theoretical concept of the community can encompass and transcend a number of spheres of interaction or integration in which not all sites are involved in the same community. Although smaller pit house sites may have been integrated with those containing the unusually large pit houses, to assume the existence of a community is premature until additional empirical data comes to light.

Sometime during the Rio de Flag phase, the Sinagua attempted to bring additional agricultural land into production away from the parks and washes. Field houses make their appearance and are sometimes associated with check dams.

In A.D. 1064 (Breternitz 1967), the initial eruption of Sunset Crater had a profound effect on the lives of the Sinagua. The phases considered here are the Angell-Winona-Padre of A.D. 1066 to 1130, the Elden phase of A.D. 1130 to 1200, the Turkey Hill phase of 1200 to 1300, and the Clear Creek phase of A.D. 1300 to 1400. Colton (1932) indicates that the ash fall from the eruption, with its moisture-retaining qualities, provided new agricultural potential, and Colton believes it was as a result of this that distant and local populations moved into the area. Breternitz (1967: 73) has also indicated the existence of a second eruption of Sunset Crater that occurred between A.D. 1066 and 1067. Recent research by Shoemaker (1977) indicates an initial eruption of Sunset Crater between A.D. 1064 and 1065 with continued, periodic, volcanic activity for the next 200 years. Increased moisture (Robinson and Dean 1969; Fish 1974), combined with the effects of the cinder mulch, ameliorated existing agricultural conditions. In addition to field houses being located in the pinyon-juniper forest, small pueblos and pit house villages began to appear along the same settlement lines as existed in the Preeruptive period. This pattern began during the Angell-Winona-Padre phase, A.D. 1066 to 1130, and continued into the Elden phase of A.D. 1130 to 1200 (see also Colton [1946]; Wilson [1969]). There is also a continuation of public works and community architecture (Madsen 1982: 18; Hudgens 1974).

During the latter part of the Angell-Winona-Padre phase, pit house village sites begin to disappear and are replaced by large aggregates of population at sites that contain both pit houses and pueblos. Wilson (1969), for example, indicates that during the Padre phase there are numerous scattered pueblos of 2 to 10 rooms throughout the Sinagua region. Ballcourts, compounds, kivalike pit houses, and community architecture were common (Wilson 1969; R. Kelly 1971b).

It is during the Posteruptive period that there is generally believed to have been a large influx of migrant populations from surrounding areas, owing to the increased farm lands created by the eruption (McGregor 1941; Colton 1946). This inference is based on a wide milieu of new cultural elements. Pilles (1979: 130) convincingly argues that this phenomenon is more apparent than real. He indicates that the increase in the number of sites results from an increased use of field houses as populations moved into the pinyon-juniper forest from the ponderosa pine forest. This is generally coincident with the Padre and Elden phases from about A.D. 1100 to 1200. Pilles (1979: 469-477) suggests that migration is only supported by a few isolated traits. Trade and the development of social hierarchies (Fish and others 1980), or what Schroeder (1965) calls "trait-unit intrusion", more likely explain the existence of intrusive cultural elements.

During the Turkey Hill phase from A.D. 1200 to 1300, the Sinagua population began to move out of the immediate Flagstaff area south and east toward Anderson Mesa (Wilson 1969; Pilles 1978). The large pueblo sites founded here include Kinnickinnick, Chavez Pass North, and the Pollock Site, all of which evidence large population aggregates.

During the Clear Creek phase, A.D. 1300 to 1400, Grapevine Pueblo and Chavez Pass South were constructed (Pilles 1978). Agriculture was intensive around Anderson Mesa, complete with field houses, terraces, and water control features (Madsen 1982: 25). Public architecture and ballcourts continue as consistent features. After about A.D. 1400 the Sinagua completely abandoned their homeland, owing to the combined effects of environmental deterioration and soil depletion.

Environment

Townsend-Divide is located at the eastern foot of Mount Elden along U.S. Highway 89, just northeast of Flagstaff (Fig. 1.1). Mount Elden is one of the silicic volcanic centers of the San Francisco Mountains volcanic field, and is approximately 8 km (5 miles) from the San Francisco Peaks (Kluth 1974: 5). The San Francisco Mountains volcanic field is one of the major volcanic areas in the United States, covering over 5200 square kilometers (2000 square miles). Most of the area's 200 cinder cones were formed during the Pleistocene, but the most recent activity occurred with the initial eruption of Sunset Crater around A.D. 1064 and 1065, which continued episodically for nearly 200 years until around A.D. 1250 (Shoemaker 1977; Pilles 1979: 459-467).

Mount Elden is made up of dacite flows, which weather down to rounded boulders that are transported down the mountain by erosion.

It is an igneous intrusion that has upturned the various sedimentary formations overlying large alluvial deposits, with intrusions of basalt and dacite that characterize the San Francisco Peaks. The strata exposed around the base of Mount Elden consist of red shales and sandstones, conglomerates, and limestone (Kluth 1974: 2; Madsen 1982: 7-8). East of Mount Elden are many other cinder cones, and four major intercone basins formed when drainages were blocked by active lava flows (Fig. 2.1). These basins are basically open expanses of alluvial deposits of rocky soils that accumulated from the San Francisco Peaks and the surrounding cinder cones (Colton 1937; Madsen 1982: 8). The four basins consist of Navajo loam, the best agricultural soil in the area, which occurs primarily in alluvial wash bottoms like the Rio de Flag and Walnut Creek, in treeless parks such as Doney and Black Bill parks, and in scattered solution-weathered pockets in the Kaibab limestone, especially in the Winona-Angell area (Pilles 1978: 120). Townsend-Divide lies on the western edge of one of the larger open basins, Doney Park. This park, and the entire locality, are drained by the Rio de Flag Creek, which enters Doney Park from the west, follows the eastern perimeter of the Turkey Hill lava flow, and eventually flows into the San Francisco Wash (Madsen 1982: 8).

Neither of the major washes nor their tributaries is a reliable water source, being dry throughout much of the year; springs provide needed water. A total of 20 springs is known below the 8000-foot contour level in the region, with at least 5 along the flanks of Mount Elden and the Peaks that have provided water since the late nineteenth century. Many of the springs are seasonal, being dependent on the amount of annual rainfall, but other, larger ones are considered almost permanent, providing the most reliable water supply in the area (Pilles 1978: 119; Madsen 1982: 8-9).

The Flagstaff region has a four-part seasonal cycle as revealed by Colton's (1958b: 1) study of modern climatic patterns. It consists of winter and summer rainy seasons, and of spring and fall dry seasons. The rainfall varies with elevation, with precipitation increasing by up to 10 inches per 1000-foot increase in elevation. The average precipitation within the ponderosa-Douglas fir zone at 6500 feet to 7400 feet (1981 m to 2255 m) elevation, which includes Townsend-Divide, is approximately 16 to 22 inches (406.4 mm to 558.8 mm) per year (Madsen 1982: 9). The growing season varies with elevation also, with the reported season for the aforementioned area between 125 and 150 frost-free days (R. Kelly 1971b: 43; Madsen 1982: 9).

Townsend-Divide, at an elevation of 6860 feet (2091 m), is located at the boundary of Doney Park, a treeless area with mixed floral associations, and the ponderosa pine forest, which occurs in pure stands between 6000 and 7000 feet (1829 m to 2134 m) and along moist drainages. The major characteristic of this community is the open understory with dominant ponderosa pine (*Pinus ponderosa*), and including dense patches of Gambel oak (*Quercus gambelli*), and scattered specimens of alligator juniper (*Juniperus deppeana*), one-seed juniper (*J. monosperma*), and pinyon pine (*P. edulis*). Grasses associated with this plant community

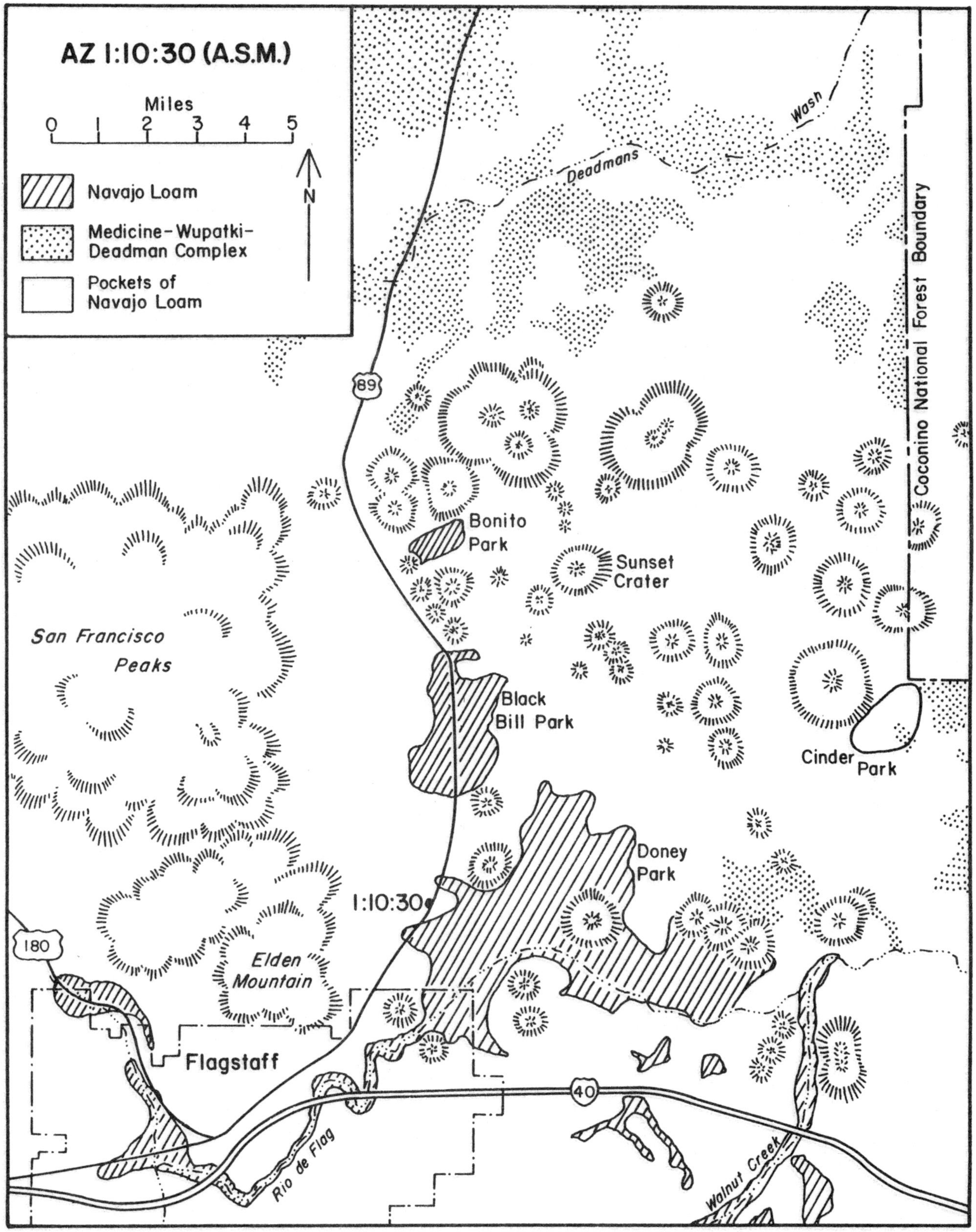

Figure 2.1 The Flagstaff area, showing cinder cones, parks, and arable soils. (after Pilles [1978: 121, Fig. 1]).

include the dominant blue grama (*Bouteloua gracilis*), black dropseed (*Sporobolus interruptus*), mountain muhly (*Muhlenbergia montana*), and common shrubs such as lemon sumac (*Rhus trilobata*), and sagebrush (*Artemisia tridentata*). Cacti are also present and include prickly pear (*Opuntia versicolor*), yucca (*Yucca baccata*), and hedgehog cactus (*Echinocereus triglochidiatus* var. *melanocanthus*) (Madsen 1982: 9-10).

A total of 56 mammal species has been identified within a 15 mile radius of Flagstaff (Hoffmeister and Carothers 1969: 184-188). The majority of these are small mammals, including various species of shrew (3), myotis (6), bat (7), prarie dog (1), squirrel (6), chipmunk (2), gopher (1), mouse (9), rat (5), vole (2), porcupine (1), raccoon (1), ringtail (1), weasel (1), ferret (1), badger (1), and skunk (1). The more commonly seen, and utilized, small mammals are the desert cottontail (*Sylvilagus audubonii*) and the black-tailed jack rabbit (*Lepus californicus*). The predominant big game today is the coyote (*Canis latrans*), gray fox (*Urocyon cinereoargenteus*), black bear (*Ursus americanus*), mountain lion (*Felis concolor*), bobcat (*Lynx rufus*), mule deer (*Odocoileus hemionus*), white-tailed deer (*O. virginianus*), and pronghorn antelope (*Antilocapra americana*). Other large mammals such as the timber wolf (*Canis lupus*), grizzly bear (*U. horribilis*), and mountain sheep (*Ovis canadensis*) were present at one time but became extinct during the nineteenth century. Also present today, but introduced in the twentieth century, are elk or wapiti (*Cervus canadensis nelsoni*).

Chapter 3

THE TOWNSEND-DIVIDE SITE (AZ I:10:30, ASM)

Field Methods

Townsend-Divide (AZ I:10:30, ASM) was tested in 1980 with three backhoe trenches, as well as intensive surface collection (Sullivan 1980). The data recovery program reported here consisted of additional backhoe trenching, and was comprised of 12 such trenches (Fig. 3.1), which were excavated from 1.5 m to 1.75 m in depth by 70 cm in width; they varied in length. All trenches were faced with a trowel to inspect for cultural features. No additional surface collection was undertaken owing to the extremely disturbed nature of the surface deposits by rodent activity and the fact that surface collection was accomplished in the testing phase.

Trench 1 was an attempt to reopen the 1980 east trench in order to relocate the pit house, the possible occupation surface, and the burial identified during the testing phase (Sullivan 1980). In addition, the north trench from the testing was reopened to ascertain the presence of a possible midden. Backhoe trenching was successful in relocating the pit house (labeled Feature 1), the burial (labeled Feature 2), and an additional pit house (labeled Feature 5), which is the occupation surface identified during testing. In addition, three inhumations (Features 3, 4, and 7) were also found in backhoe trenches (Fig. 3.2).

After all features were located, an arbitrary grid system tied into the datum from testing was superimposed over the site area that was within the highway realignment. The datum was designated 100 North/100 East and served as the horizontal control reference. All excavation units were designated by their southwest corner. Vertical control was maintained with reference to a datum placed in a billboard approximately 1 m above the ground surface.

Feature excavation techniques were quite simple. In the pit houses an initial, exploratory, 2-m-by-2-m test unit was excavated in 50-cm levels from the existing ground surface to the floor of the structure. Due to time considerations and the homogeneity and depth of the fill in the pit houses, approximately 1 m of fill in each pit house was mechanically removed by a backhoe. Grab samples were collected from the backhoe backdirt while all hand-excavated earth was passed through a quarter-inch wire mesh screen. All artifactual material was bagged

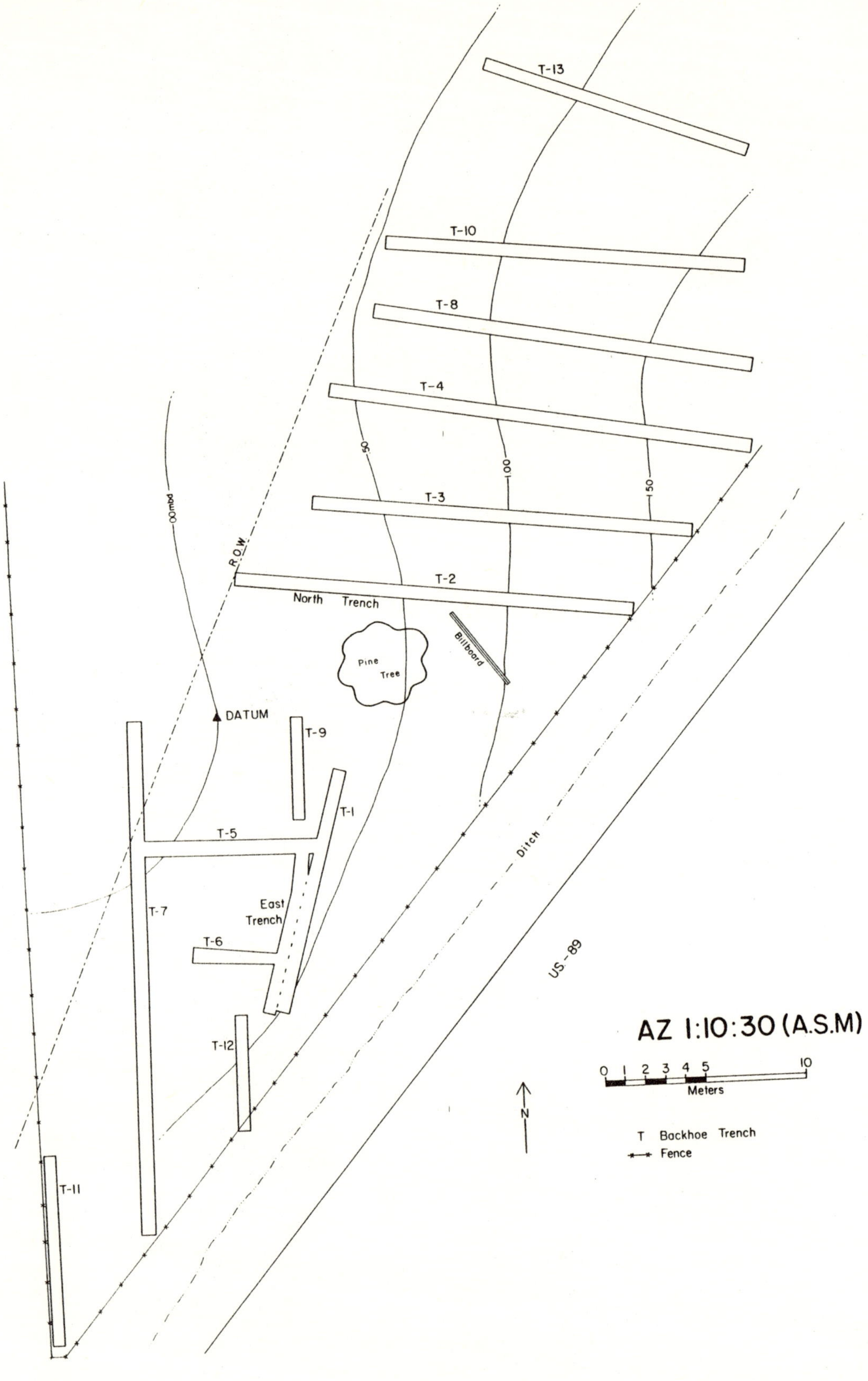

Figure 3.1 Distribution of backhoe trenches at Townsend-Divide.

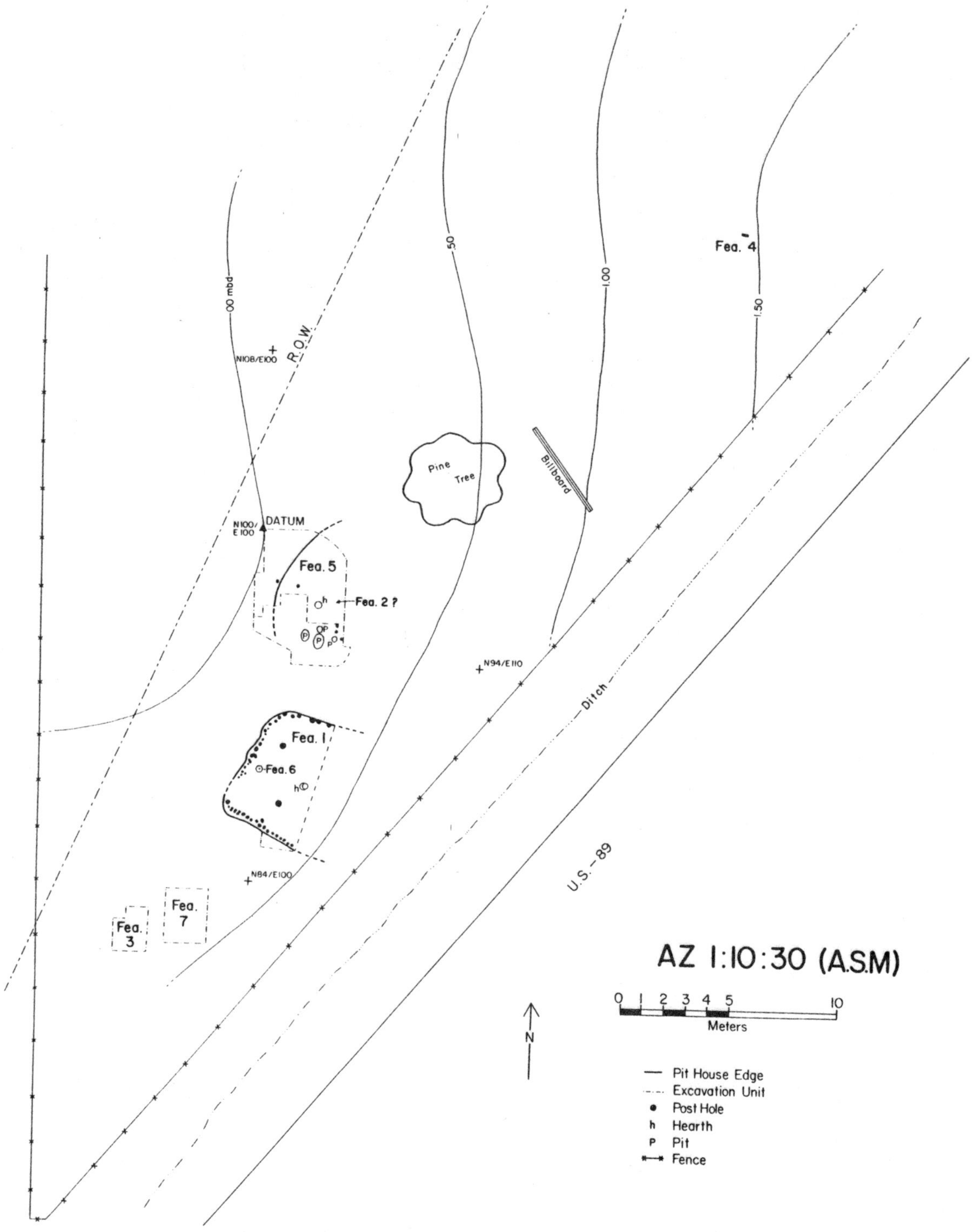

Figure 3.2 Site map of Townsend-Divide.

with reference to provenience, feature, stratum, level, and depth as applicable. Flotation samples were collected from each hand-excavated level as well as from floor features. Internal features within each pit house were decimalized. For example, a hearth in Feature 1 was designated Feature 1.1.

Excavation of the inhumations was also straightforward. As all but one were found in backhoe trenches and no burial pits were in evidence (all were placed into trash deposits), a 2-m-by-2-m unit was placed over the burial and excavated in 20-cm levels. All material was passed through quarter-inch wire mesh screen.

Photographs, plan views, and profiles were made for each feature upon completion of the excavation. All features were transferred to the master contour map, and all information was recorded on standardized Arizona State Museum forms. Archaeomagnetic samples were collected from the three hearths that were present.

Site Stratigraphy

The general stratigraphy at Townsend-Divide is quite simple, consisting of three strata. The uppermost stratum from the present ground surface is about 70 cm to 80 cm thick. It consists of a dark brown loamy colluvium (Navajo loam?) that is mixed with dacite cobbles, gravels, and abundant artifactual material; it qualifies as sheet trash. Below this is a 30-cm to 40-cm stratum consisting of a sterile, reddish-orange silt mixed with abundant dacite cobbles. The cobbles most likely result from erosional episodes of Mount Elden and the foothills above Townsend-Divide. This dacite substratum is common throughout the area (DeBoer 1980: 15). Below this is a sterile, reddish-orange consolidated silt stratum. Its thickness is unknown, as the backhoe trenching terminated at this level. Toward the northern portion of the site (Fig. 3.1) the dacite cobble stratum is within 40 cm of the present ground surface. Figure 3.3 illustrates the stratigraphic sequence at Townsend-Divide.

Architectural Features

Two pit houses comprise the extant sample of architectural features excavated at Townsend-Divide. They are described below.

Feature 1, Pit House (Fig. 3.4)

Shape and Dimensions. This structure is rectangular or squarish, the east wall having been removed by a backhoe trench. It measures approximately 7 m (north-south) by 5 m (east-west).

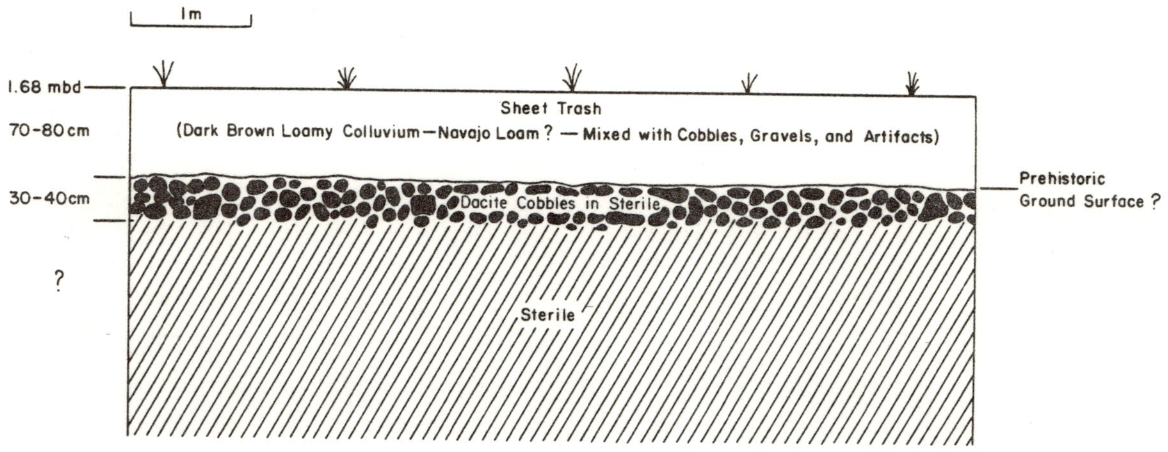

Figure 3.3 Profile of Townsend-Divide stratigraphy.

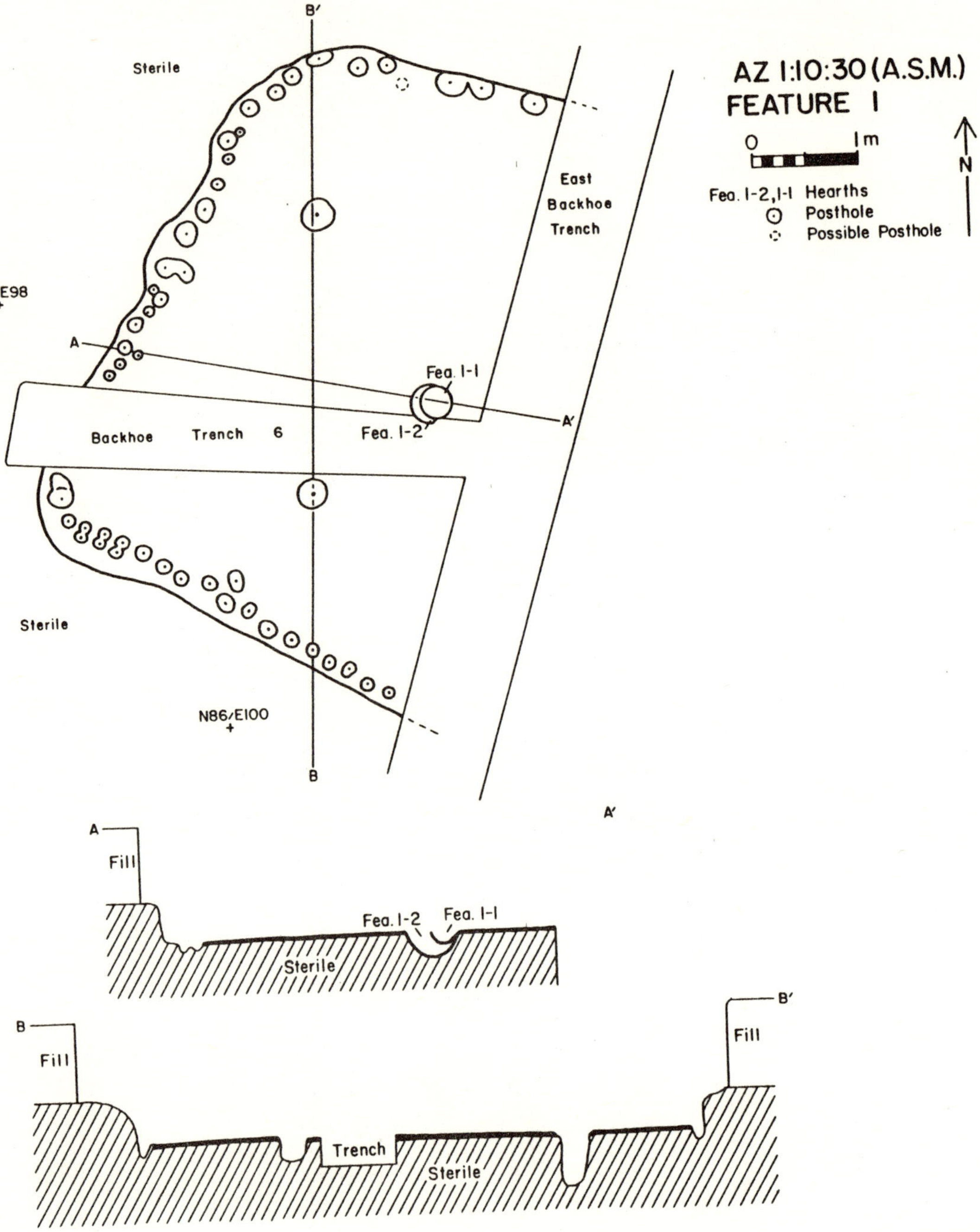

Figure 3.4 Plan View and profile of Feature 1, a pit house.

Floor. Designated as Stratum 20, it was constructed of clay plaster over the native sterile substrate. Three episodes of replastering were indicated by hearth remodeling and capping (see below).

Side Walls. The walls of the house pit are approximately 40 cm of native sterile soil. Placed against the pit walls were 40 postholes forming the side walls of the structure, which was most likely jacal.

Entry. No evidence of an entry was preserved. Given the location of the hearth, however, the entry may have been in the midsection of the east wall or through the roof.

Fill. Designated as Stratum 1, it consisted of approximately 1.4 m of gray-brown sandy silt. Abundant artifactual material (trash?) is mixed with large cobbles (erosional material from Mount Elden), volcanic cinders, and gravels.

Hearth. Two hearths were present; the upper hearth was designated as Feature 1.1 and the lower hearth was designated as Feature 1.2. Feature 1.2, the lower hearth, is a circular, clay-lined pit (38 cm in diameter by 16 cm deep). It contained four stata which were, from bottom to top: dark gray ash, white vitrified ash, brown sandy loam, and oxidized reddish clay. Feature 1.1, the upper hearth, was built inside Feature 1.2. Feature 1.1 is a circular, clay-lined pit (28 cm in diameter by 10 cm deep). The fill in this hearth consisted of a dark brown loamy silt with a thin ash lens. Feature 1.1 was capped with clay floor plaster suggesting that a third hearth was probably present, although it may have been removed by a backhoe trench. Feature 1.1 returned a first option archaeomagnetic date of A.D. 970 to 1090 and a second option of A.D. 1060 to 1340 (both at the 95 percent confidence level; the 63 percent confidence level and best fit are listed in Appendix E). Feature 1.2 returned a single option archaeomagnetic date of A.D. 1000 to 1090 (95 percent confidence level; the 63 percent confidence level and best fit are listed in Appendix E).

Floor Features. Two large circular roof support postholes (Features 1.36 and 1.37) are centrally located, and 40 smaller circular postholes encircle the floor against the pit wall.

Intrusive Features. Feature 6, an inhumation, was recovered in the fill of Feature 1, approximately 40 cm above the floor surface (see below).

Feature 5, Pit House (Fig. 3.5)

Shape and Dimensions. This cannot be determined as a result of extensive root, rodent, and erosional disturbance. Extent of the floor remnant is approximately 6 m (north-south) by 3 m (east-west).

Side Walls. Unknown; no evidence preserved.

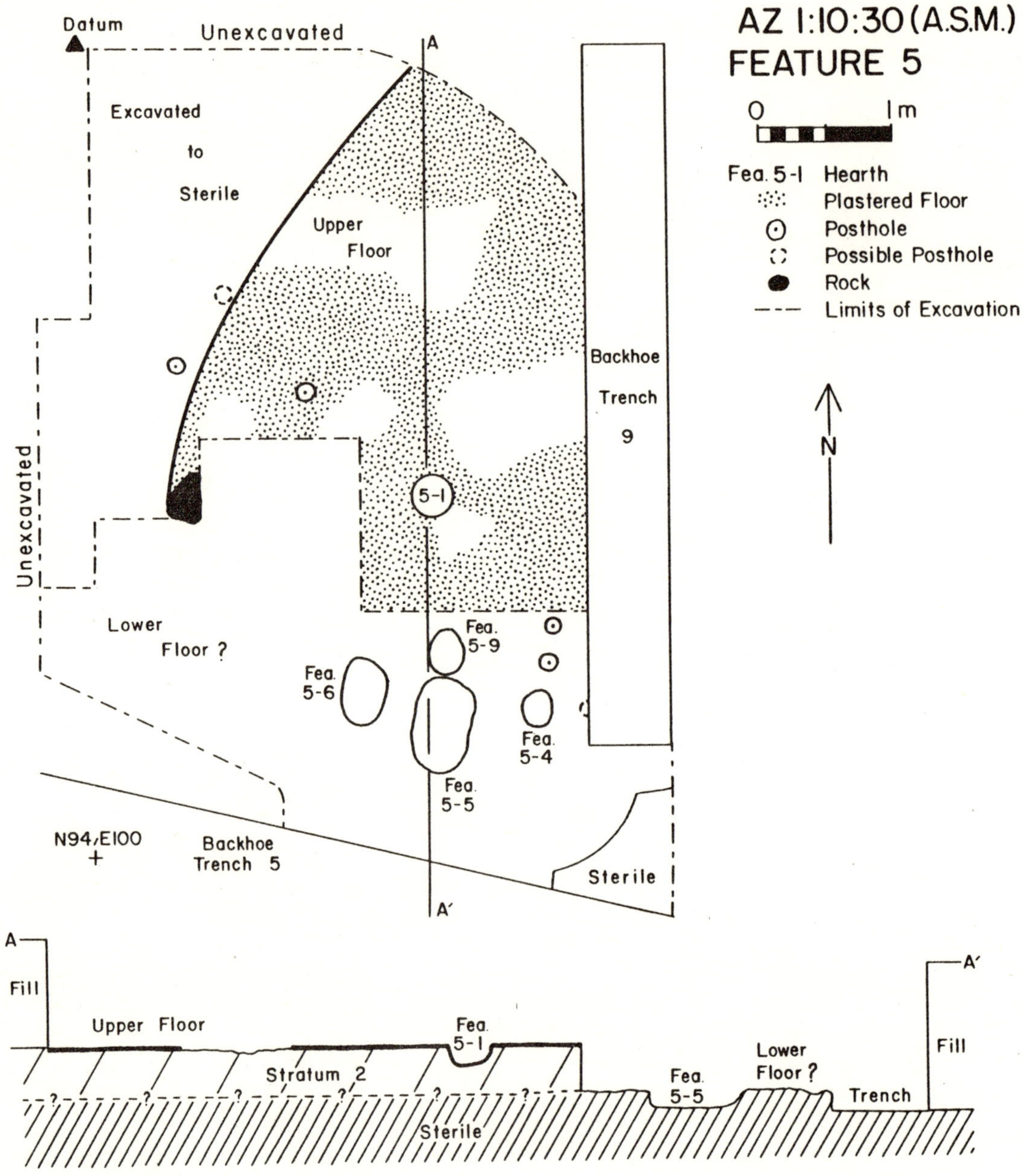

Figure 3.5 Plan view and profile of Feature 5, a pit house.

Floor. Possibly two were present. The upper floor surface was designated as Stratum 20 and was constructed of clay plaster. It was heavily eroded. The lower floor, Stratum 21, approximately 50 cm lower, apparently was compacted native sterile soil. It was not completely excavated.

Fill. Two strata were present. Stratum 1 is approximately 1.0 m of dark brown, unconsolidated loamy silt, which lies above Stratum 20, the upper floor. Stratum 1 contained abundant artifactual material, volcanic cinders, and medium-to-large cobbles. Stratum 2 is 50 cm of fill between Stratum 20 and Stratum 21, the lower floor. It consisted of reddish-orange gravelly silt and contained sparse artifactual material, cinders, gravels, and large cobbles.

Hearth. A circular, clay-lined pit (34 cm in diamter by 15 cm deep) was located in the upper floor and designated Feature 5.1. Fill consisted of dark brown gravelly silt. No hearth was found in the excavated portion of Stratum 21. Feature 5.1 returned a first option archaeomagnetic date of A.D. 1000 to 1090 and a second option of A.D. 1060 to 1270 (both at the 95 percent confidence level; the 63 percent confidence level and best fit are provided in Appendix E).

Floor Features. The upper floor contained two postholes (Features 5.2 and 5.3); the lower floor contained four pits and two postholes.

Feature 5.4 is a circular pit (30 cm in diamter by 43 cm deep) with a brown, sterile fill. Its function is not known.

Feature 5.5 is an oval, basin-shaped pit (70 cm by 47 cm by 10 cm deep). The fill consisted of a gray-brown silt. Its function is not known.

Feature 5.6 is an oval, straight-sided pit (50 cm by 42 cm by 22 cm deep). Its fill consisted of orangish-brown sandy silt. Its function is not known.

Feature 5.7 is a possible posthole.

Feature 5.8 is a posthole.

Feature 5.9 is an oval, straight-sided pit (37 cm by 27 cm by 28 cm deep). The fill consisted of a sterile brown silt. Its function is not known.

Intrusive Features. Feature 2, a disturbed burial, was recovered from the fill of the pit house (see below).

Discussion

Because only two pit houses were encountered in the portion of Townsend-Divide discussed in this report, and one of these (Feature 5) was extremely disturbed, architectural comparisons are severely restricted.

The extant portion of Feature 1, however, does appear to be architecturally similar to other pit houses reported from the Flagstaff area. For example, it appears to be similar to the alcove house at Jack Smith's Alcove Site, NA 408A (Colton 1946: 63, Fig. 32), a site occupied during the Rio de Flag phase in which encircling postholes are present. In his general treatment of Sinagua architecture, Colton illustrates two architectural styles that are prevalent during the Rio de Flag phase. Feature 1 shares affinites with both types, but it must be recalled that the east side of Feature 1 is missing due to the backhoe trench excavated during testing (Sullivan [1980], east trench) and our attempt (Trench 1) to reopen that trench. Nonetheless, the encircling postholes and two internal support postholes suggest that Feature 1 may have been a timber pit house (Colton 1946: 268, Fig. 152).

From the Winona phase, McGregor (1941: 91, Fig. 27) illustrates a pit house from NA 2133A that he suggests is Hohokam-like in its architectural attributes. Pilles (1979) has suggested that although Hohokam attributes are not uncommon among the Sinagua, they represent intrusions of the traits themselves rather than an influx of Hohokam peoples. At NA 2135C, an Angell phase site, McGregor (1941; 102, Fig. 33) illustrates an alcove pit house with encircling posts. This pit house, however, had an elevated bench into which posts were set. As field time at Townsend-Divide did not permit external stripping around Feature 1, it is unknown whether a bench was present into which roofing beams may have been set.

At the more recently excavated Pershing Site, NA 7207, Wilson illustrates two pit houses, B (1969: 64, Fig. 3) and L (1969: 111, Fig. 13), that are similar to Feature 1. Structure B is estimated by Wilson to date between A.D. 1025 and 1075, while Structure L is estimated between A.D. 1050 and 1080--his late Ceramic Group III to Ceramic Group IV. These dates correspond to the late Rio de Flag phase and Angell-Winona phases.

Based on these limited comparative data, Feature 1 is most likely the remnant of an architectural style that begins during the Rio de Flag phase and continues short-lived into the Angell-Winona phases. Its encircling postholes, its depth below the prehistoric ground surface, and its arrangement of internal support postholes (Fig. 3.4), are the data on which this inference is based. In some respects there are similarities in this architectural style with Hohokam houses of the Sedentary period.

Burials

The remains of six individuals, and some scattered, nonburial context human remains were recovered from Townsend-Divide. The six individuals were in five distinct features; two of the six were included in a multiple burial. For more detailed osteological information on the burials, refer to Appendix A.

Feature 2

Feature 2 was located in the east backhoe trench during the 1980 testing of the site. It consisted of an Angell Brown bowl resting within a Winona Brown bowl, associated with some human teeth and a mandible observed behind it. There was no evidence of a burial pit, and the remains were resting on sterile soil (Sullivan 1980: 33-36, Fig. 13). The burial was not specifically relocated during the recent excavations, but the scattered remains of a child between 6 and 18 months old (Burial 5) and an assortment of artifacts, including two Early Angell Brown miniature bowls (see Fig. 3.7*a*, *c*), two complete obsidian projectile points (see Fig. 3.14*e*, *h*), and two ornaments (see Figs. 3.16*e* and 3.17*j*), were recovered in the fill of Feature 5 where the burial was thought to be located. It seems probable that the burial was interred in the fill of the pit house, or perhaps on the floor of the structure since it was reported to be resting on a sterile surface, and has been heavily disturbed through time by natural or cultural agents.

Feature 3

Feature 3 consisted of two adult females interred together in the sheet trash of the site, 6 m southwest of Feature 1, a pit house (Fig. 3.2). Individual B (Burial 2) was lying on its right side in a semiflexed position, facing east and with the head to the south. Individual A (Burial 1) was lying over Individual B, fully extended on its back, with the right arm crossed over the torso and the legs crossed at the knees. The body was oriented to the south, with its head resting on the head of Individual B, and its feet resting on the feet of the lower body (Fig. 3.6). There appears to have been no disturbance to the lower body when the upper body was interred, suggesting that they were interred at the same time. No grave goods were found with the burial, although a complete three-quarter grooved axe (see Fig. 3.15*e*) was found in the backdirt of Backhoe Trench 7, from the vicinity of the grave, and may have been associated with it. There was no indication of a defined grave pit: the individuals were lying on sterile substrate in cultural sheet trash.

Feature 4

Feature 4 appeared to be a burial almost totally destroyed by Backhoe Trench 4, approximately 18 m northeast of Feature 5; only one ulna and radius remained undisturbed in the north wall of the trench. The individual (Burial 6) was a subadult aged 15 years. No grave goods

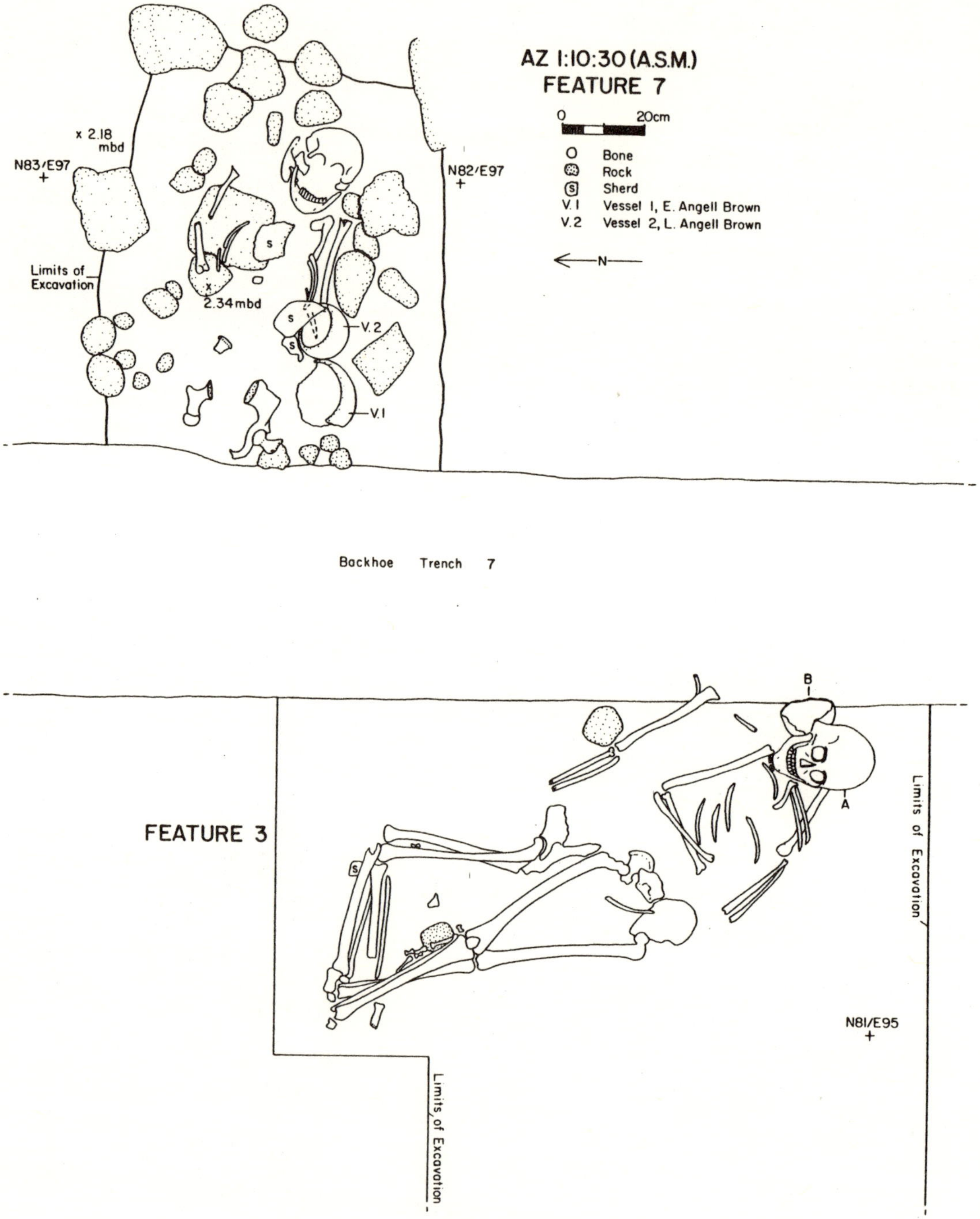

Figure 3.6 Plan views of Features 3 and 7 (Burials 1, 2, and 3, respectively).

were encountered, and no burial pit was noted. The individual appeared to have been interred in cultural sheet trash, and was lying on sterile soil.

Feature 6

Feature 6 was very similar to Feature 2, consisting of various grave goods and scattered human bone in the fill of Feature 1, a pit house. The artifacts thought to be associated include an early Angell Brown bowl with a Turkey Hill Red (on early Angell Brown) jar inside (see Fig. 3.7f-g), and a sherd cover, a miniature, early Angell Brown jar (see Fig. 3.7h), four obsidian projectile points (see Fig. 3.14a-c, f), a complete shell bracelet (see Fig. 3.17i), and a shell earring. The human bone recovered in the vicinity of the artifacts (Burial 4) are from a child aged 6 to 18 months. No pit was discernable, and the remains were 40 cm above the pit house floor, apparently interred after the house was abandoned and had started to fill in with trash and natural deposition.

Feature 7

Feature 7 (Burial 3) was the remains of a female aged 25 to 35 years, buried less than 1 m east of the Feature 3 burials. The burial had been heavily disturbed both by natural agents and by Backhoe Trench 7 (which removed the legs), and very little remained intact. It was fully extended on its back with the head to the east (Fig. 3.6). Two vessels, one complete late Angell Brown bowl (see Fig. 3.7e) and a partially reconstructable early Angell Brown bowl (see Fig. 3.7d) were placed by the left side of the body, just above the innominates. Remains of another vessel were scattered on top of the body. It is possible that the three-quarter grooved axe described in the Feature 3 discussion could have been associated with this burial. There was no evidence of a grave pit as the burial was interred in cultural sheet trash.

Nonfeature Remains

Finally, 12 additional human bones were recovered from nonburial contexts. These include four bones from the upper fill of Feature 3 which probably belong to Burial 1 or 2, one femur fragment from Backhoe Trench 7 backdirt that probably belongs to Burial 3, four bones (including two cremated) from the fill of Feature 1, two rib fragments from the fill of Feature 5 which may belong to Burial 5, and a cremated adult bone from the Feature 6 burial (see Table A.1).

Discussion

Of the five burial features recorded, three can be temporally placed because of associated artifacts (consisting of ceramic vessels in all cases). With the exception of what was identified as a Winona Brown bowl by Sullivan (1980) and the Turkey Hill Red jar from Feature 6, all pottery associated with the burials was early or late Angell Brown, including five bowls and two miniature bowls. This would place the burials in the late Rio de Flag phase (around A.D. 1000-1066) or early Angell phase (A.D. 1064-1100). There appears to be no well-defined cemetery, the bodies having been placed throughout the site area.

Extended burials with offerings were the normal mode of disposal of the dead for the Sinagua, lasting throughout their prehistory. Some loosely flexed and a few tightly flexed inhumations are also seen, which may have been influenced by the Kayenta Anasazi. Cremation, thought to have been influenced by the Hohokam, was introduced after A.D. 1070 in the Winona phase, but did not last long in the Flagstaff area (Colton 1946: 295). Hohman (1982: 40) indicates the possibility, however, that cremation might have been practiced in Preeruptive times, significantly prior to any major contact with people from the south. Hohman (1982: 41-42) also suggests that age, sex, and social status were important factors in mortuary treatment. Subadults consistently yielded fewer mortuary offerings in his study, although this does not hold true for Townsend-Divide if Features 2 and 6 were indeed subadult burials. Females from the Angell-Winona phase generally received fewer offerings than males and in those instances where offerings were present, they consisted mainly of ground stone (such as manos and metates), limited ceramics (generally plain wares), and shell, which could reflect personal items of the deceased. Finally, the type of grave, clay lined versus a simple hole, is thought to be an indicator of status, and mass burials (two or more bodies in one grave) with no offerings, are not uncommon for low status individuals (Hohman 1982: 61). If these factors hold true, the fact that both Features 3 and 7 contained females might explain the two individuals and lack of offerings in Feature 3 and the plain ware vessels in Feature 7, as well as the lack of a prepared burial pit in both cases. It would also suggest that Feature 6 was a higher status burial, with at least nine offerings (including carved shell). This deviation from the norm of few offerings with subadults was thought to reflect the status of the adult male of the household (Hohman 1982: 61).

Before A.D. 1070, the dead were buried in various areas throughout the site, in any place where the digging was easy, preferably in abandoned rooms or in trash areas; after A.D. 1070, there appeared to have been definite cemeteries, usually in trash mounds, which were used by people throughout the occupation of the site (McGregor 1941: 271-273; Colton 1946: 294). Other than that variation through time, there does not appear to be any correlation between phases, burial position, and the presence or absence of offerings (McGregor 1941: 274). McGregor (1941: 271) also noted at Winona Village features such as Features 2 and 6 at Townsend-Divide, which consist of odd bones and small ceramic vessels in trash mounds. He explained them as graves in which all or most of the bones were destroyed by rodents such as wood rats or pack rats, leaving only vessels as a mark of former inhumations.

The Artifact Assemblage

Ceramics

The first part of this section details the analysis of the Alameda Brown Wares recovered during excavations at Townsend-Divide. Locally produced ceramics comprised approximately 93.6 percent of the total ceramic assemblage (n=6534; see Table 3.1). All brown ware types fit classifications described by Colton and Hargrave (1937), and Colton (1955, 1956, 1958a).

Alameda Brown Ware is the term given to the ". . . principle utilty and service ware of the Sinagua. . . ." (Colton 1946: 34). These types were manufactured from residual basaltic clays and crushed crystalline rock from the San Francisco Peaks area, constructed by the paddle and anvil method, and fired in an oxidizing atmosphere. Alameda Brown Wares persisted through 700 years of prehistory with a range that extended north to Deadman's Wash, east to Meteor Crater, south to the Verde Valley, and west to the San Francisco Peaks.

For the purposes of this study, the types Angell Brown and Turkey Hill Red on Angell Brown were subdivided into early and late groupings. Qualitative research in the Flagstaff area, specifically by the Coconino National Forest, Flagstaff, Arizona, has attempted to further refine the A.D. 900 to 1100 period (Rio de Flag, Angell-Winona, Padre phases) through analyses of slight temper differences in Angell Brown. At present, these distinctions are limited to a qualitative assessment of the amount and size of crushed volcanic tuff visible in cross section. Early Angell Brown is more like Rio de Flag Brown with sanidine crystals, and small amounts of fine volcanic tuff as temper. Late Angell Brown is more like Winona Brown, with no sanidine crystals, and still small, though more abundant, amounts of volcanic tuff as temper. Angell Brown was originally introduced as an intergrade between Rio de Flag Brown and Winona Brown and was considered unimportant as a temporal indicator (Colton and Hargrave 1937; Colton 1946: 26). These groupings may prove valid when brown ware frequencies are compared with intrusive white wares and red wares of the same period, perhaps suggesting that Angell Brown can be a significant temporal indicator.

Researchers with the Coconino National Forest have found that ceramic groups assigned an A.D. 1067 to 1130 time frame, or Wilson's (1969: Table 20) Group IV, can be further subdivided based on the occurrence of certain white wares in association with either early or late Angell Brown. It appears that Black Mesa Black-on-white, Rio de Flag Brown and Angell Brown, and, in smaller quantities, Winona Brown, occur during the Angell-Winona phase (A.D. 1066-1100), contrasted with a decreased percentage of Angell Brown and increased amounts of Winona Brown and Sunset Brown during Padre phase times (A.D. 1100-1130). The earliest appearance of Angell Brown, possibly early Angell (as defined here), occurs during the Rio de Flag phase (A.D. 900 or 950-1066).

Unfortunately, these inferences remain largely unsubstantiated due to a lack of systematic, quantitative analyses. However, field studies suggest further in-depth investigations are necessary and worthwhile.

Alameda Brown Wares

Seven different Alameda Brown Ware types were identified at Townsend-Divide (Table 3.1).

Rio de Flag Brown was represented by 20 jar sherds and 49 bowl sherds, of which 2 were jar rims and 5 were bowl rims (0.98 percent). Twenty-one percent of the bowls were smudged, which is interesting considering that jars are the predominant form in Rio de Flag Brown (Colton and Hargrave 1937). Perhaps, if a larger Rio de Flag Brown sample was obtained, the ratio of bowls to jars would change, as well as the percentage of smudged variety, approximating that of both early and late Angell Brown.

Not surprisingly, Angell Brown was the most common type, with 6418 sherds, or 91.9 percent of the ceramic assemblage. Late Angell Brown, defined here as a variety of Colton's Angell Brown, comprised 4425 sherds, or 63.4 percent of all ceramics, with jar forms represented by 2716 sherds (104 rims) and bowls with 1709 sherds (146 rims). The late Angell smudged bowl variety had 457 sherds, or 10.3 percent of the late Angell population. Early Angell Brown constituted 1993 sherds (28.5 percent) with jars again the dominant form, although to a lesser degree; 1105 jar sherds (61 rims) and 88 bowl sherds (98 rims) were present. Of the 888 early Angell bowl sherds, 225 exhibited smudging. Smudged ware is defined here as a sooted, polished variety common to plain ware bowl interiors. Unfortunately, the smudged variety appeared in an assortment of levels and did not occur within any particular context.

Key to Ceramic Tables

J	Jar form sherds
B	Bowl form sherds
/	Rim sherds/body sherds
[ ]	Excavation stratum
( )	Smudged sherds

Table 3.1

CERAMIC TYPES (SHERDS) FROM TOWNSEND-DIVIDE (AZ I:10:30, ASM)

Provenience	Alameda Brown Wares: Rio de Flag Brown J	B	Early Angell Brown J	B	Late Angell Brown J	B	Winona Brown J	B	Youngs Brown J	B	Sunset Brown J	B	Turkey Hill Red (on Early Angell) J	B	Turkey Hill Red (on Late Angell) J	B	Grapevine Red J	B
Feature 1																		
Fill [S1]	0/8	0/12 (2)	27/567	46/316 (85)	54/1480	73/723 (194)	0/10	1/5 (3)	0	0	0	0	0	0	1/0	0/6	0	0
Floor[S20]	0	0	0/2	1/3	2/10	1/14 (6)	0	0	0	0	0	0	0	0	0	0	0	0
Feature 1.1	0	0	0	0	0/1	0	0	0	0	0	0	0	0	0	0	0	0	0
Feature 1.2	0	0	0	0/3	1/3	0/2 (1)	0	0	0	0	0	0	0	0	0	0	0	0
Feature 1.28	0	0	0	0	0/2	0	0	0	0	0	0	0	0	0	0	0	0	0
Feature 1.29	0	0	0	0	0/1	0	0	0	0	0	0	0	0	0	0	0	0	0
Feature 1.30	0	0	0	0	0	0/1	0	0	0	0	0	0	0	0	0	0	0	0
Feature 2	0	0/1 (1)	2/22	1/6 (1)	0/37	2/12 (3)	0	0	0	0	0	0	0	0	0	0	0	0
Feature 3	0	0	0/15	3/19 (9)	1/34	0/16 (8)	0	0	0	0	0	0	0	0	0	0	0	0
Feature 5																		
Fill [S1]	2/8	4/27 (7)	26/401	43/403 (118)	44/964	65/721 (227)	0/2	0/3 (3)	0/1	1/0	0	0/2 (2)	0	1/3	0	0/1	0	0
Floor [S20]	0	0	0	0	0	0	0	0	0	0	0	0	0	0	0	0	0	0
Fill [S2]	0/1	0/3	5/18	0/21 (6)	1/36	1/31 (8)	0	0	0	0	0	0/2 (2)	0	0	0	0	0	0
Floor [S21]	0	0	0	0	0	0	0	0	0	0	0	0	0	0	0	0	0	0
Feature 5.1	0	0/1	0/1	0	0	0	0	0	0	0	0	0	0	0	0	0	0	0
Feature 5.3	0	1/0	0	0	0	0	0	0	0	0	0	0	0	0	0	0	0	
Feature 5.4	0	0	0	0	0/2	0/1	0	0	0	0	0	0	0	0	0	0	0	0
Feature 5.5	0	0	0	0	0/2	0/1	0	0	0	0	0	0	0	0	0	0	0	0
Feature 5.6	0	0	0	1/0	0	0	0	0	0	0	0	0	0	0	0	0	0	0
Feature 5.9	0	0	0	0	0	0/1	0	0	0	0	0	0	0	0	0	0	0	0
Feature 6	0/1	0	0/6	0/4	0	0/1	0	0	0	0	0	0	0	0	0	0	0	0
Feature 7	0/0	0	1/6	1/5 (3)	1/16	2/30 (5)	0	0/2	0	0	0	0	0	0	0	0	0	0/2
Trench 1	0	0	0/2	2/5 (1)	0/10	0/1	0	0	0	0	0	0	0	0	0	0	0	0
Trench 2	0	0	0/4	0/5 (2)	0/14	2/8 (5)	0	0	0	0	0	0	0	0	0	1/1	0	0
Subtotal	2/18	5/44 (12)	61/1044	98/790 (225)	104/2612	146/1563 (457)	0/12	1/10 (6)	0/1	1/0	0/0	0/4 (4)	0/0	1/3	1/0	1/8	0/0	0/2
TOTAL	69		1993		4425		23		2		4		4		10		2	

Winona Brown, with 23 sherds (0.3 percent), was almost equally divided between jars (12, or 53 percent) and bowls (11, or 48.0 percent), of which almost one-half of the bowl sherds were smudged. Only one rim sherd from a bowl was present. A scant two sherds (0.03 percent) comprised the Youngs Brown subtype: one jar body sherd and one bowl rim sherd. Sunset Brown consisted of four bowl body sherds (0.05 percent). A single bowl rim sherd and three bowl body sherds (0.05 percent) constituted Turkey Hill Red on early Angell Brown, while one jar rim, one bowl rim, and eight bowl body sherds (0.14 percent) of Turkey Hill Red were on late Angell Brown. Only two body sherds (0.03 percent) of Grapevine Red were present at Townsend-Divide.

Eleven whole or reconstructable vessels (Fig. 3.7) were recovered. A partially reconstructable late Angell Brown jar was found on the floor of Feature 1, a pit house. The excavation level just above the floor contained a fragment of a miniature late Angell Brown bowl.

Two miniature early Angell Brown bowls were recovered from the fill of Feature 5, a pit house (Fig. 3.7a, c). They were most likely associated with Feature 2, a burial intrusive into the fill of Feature 5. The bowls are discussed with Feature 2. A Winona Brown bowl (Fig. 3.7b) and a partial Angell Brown bowl, also associated with this feature, were recovered during testing (Sullivan 1980).

A complete late Angell Brown bowl (Fig. 3.7g), a complete Turkey Hill Red (on early Angell Brown) jar (Fig. 3.7f), and a miniature, early Angell Brown jar (Fig. 3.7h) were found in association with Feature 6, a burial intrusive into the fill of Feature 1, a pit house. These vessels are described with Feature 6.

A partially reconstructable early Angell Brown bowl (Fig. 3.7d), and two partially reconstructable late Angell Brown bowls (Fig. 3.7e) were found in association with the fill of Feature 7, a burial. They are discussed with that feature.

Although a comprehensive examination of vessel forms was not undertaken, gross classifications were noted. Jars, as mentioned, comprised the majority of Alameda Brown Wares. These sherds displayed recurved rims with flat or rounded lips characterisitic of globular, ollalike vessels. The rim sherds conformed to Colton's (1941: 66) classes IB3 or IB4 and IC3 or IC4. Bowls, generally straight sided with flat or rounded lips, were similar to Classes IA3 and IA4. Two late Angell Brown seed jars were also represented; their rims were most like those of Class ID4.

Tusayan White Wares

Six pottery types associated with Tusayan White Wares (Table 3.2) were present at Townsend-Divide (Fig. 3.8); accounting for 1.49 percent of the sample (n=104). Black Mesa Black-on-white (Fig. 3.8d) was represented by 16 sherds (0.23 percent), with 2 jar forms and

Figure 3.7 Whole and reconstructable vessels from Townsend-Divide. a, c, d, h, early Angell Brown; e, g, late Angell Brown; b, Winona Brown; f, Turkey Hill Red (height of e is 11.1 cm).

Table 3.2

CERAMIC TYPES (SHERDS FROM TOWNSEND-DIVIDE (AZ I:10:30, ASM)

Tusayan White Wares and Tusayan Gray Wares

Provenience	Black Mesa B/W		Black Mesa/Sosi B/W		Sosi B/W		Dogoszhi B/W		Flagstaff B/W		Shato B/W		Unidentified Tusayan White Ware		Medicine Gray		Tusayan Corrugated	
	J	B	J	B	J	B	J	B	J	B	J	B	J	B	J	B	J	B
Feature 1	1/0	0/5	0/3	3/5	0	1/0	0	1/0	0	2/4	0	0/3	0/9	1/14	0	0/1	1/25	0
Fill [S1]	0	0	0	0	0	0	0	0	0	0	0	0	0/8	0	0	0	0	0
Floor [S2]	0	0	0	0	0	0	0	0	0	0	0	0	0	0	0	0	0	0
Feature 1.1	0	0	0	0	0	0	0	0	0	0	0	0	0	0	0	0	0/1	0
Feature 1.2	0	0	0	0	0	0	0	0	0	0	0	0	0	0	0	0	0	0
Feature 1.28	0	0	0	0	0	0	0	0	0	0	0	0	0	0	0	0	0	0
Feature 1.29	0	0	0	0	0	0	0	0	0	0	0	0	0	0	0	0	0	0
Feature 1.30	0	0	0	0	0	0	0	0	0	0	0	0	0	0	0	0	0	0
Feature 2	0/1	0	0	0	0	0	0	0	0	0	0	0	0	0	0	0	0	0
Feature 3	0	0	0	0	0	0	0/1	0	0	0	0	0	0	0	0	0	0/1	0
Feature 5																		
Fill [S1]	0	1/7	0	4/2	0	0/6	0	0	0	1/0	0	1/0	2/1	0/13	0	0	7/24	0
Floor [S20]	0	0	0	0	0	0	0	0	0	0	0	0	0	0	0	0	0	0
Fill [S2]	0	0	0	0	0	0	0	0/1	0	0	0	0/1	0	0	0	0	0/1	0
Floor [S21]	0	0	0	0	0	0	0	0	0	0	0	0	0	0	0	0	0	0
Feature 5.1	0	0	0	0	0	0	0	0	0	0	0	0	0	0	0	0	0	0
Feature 5.3	0	0	0	0	0	0	0	0	0	0	0	0	0	0	0	0	0	0
Feature 5.4	0	0	0	0	0	0	0	0	0	0	0	0	0	0	0	0	0	0
Feature 5.5	0	0	0	0	0	0	0	0	0	0	0	0	0	0	0	0	0	0
Feature 5.6	0	0	0	0	0	0	0	0	0	0	0	0	0	0	0	0	0	0
Feature 5.9	0	0	0	0	0	0	0	0	0	0	0	0	0	0	0	0	0	0
Feature 6	0	0	0	0	0	0	0	0	0	0	0	0	0	0	0	0	0	0
Feature 7	0	0/1	0/1	0	0	0	0	0	0	0	0	0	0	0	0	0	0	0
Trench 1	0	0	0	0	0	0	0	0	0	0	0	0	0	0	0	0	0	0
Trench 2	0	0	0	0	0	0	0	0	0	0	0	0	0	0	0	0	0	0
Subtotal	1/1	1/13	0/4	7/7	0	1/6	0/1	1/1	0	3/4	0	1/4	2/18	1/27	0	0/1	8/52	0
TOTAL	16		18		7		3		4		5		48		1		60	

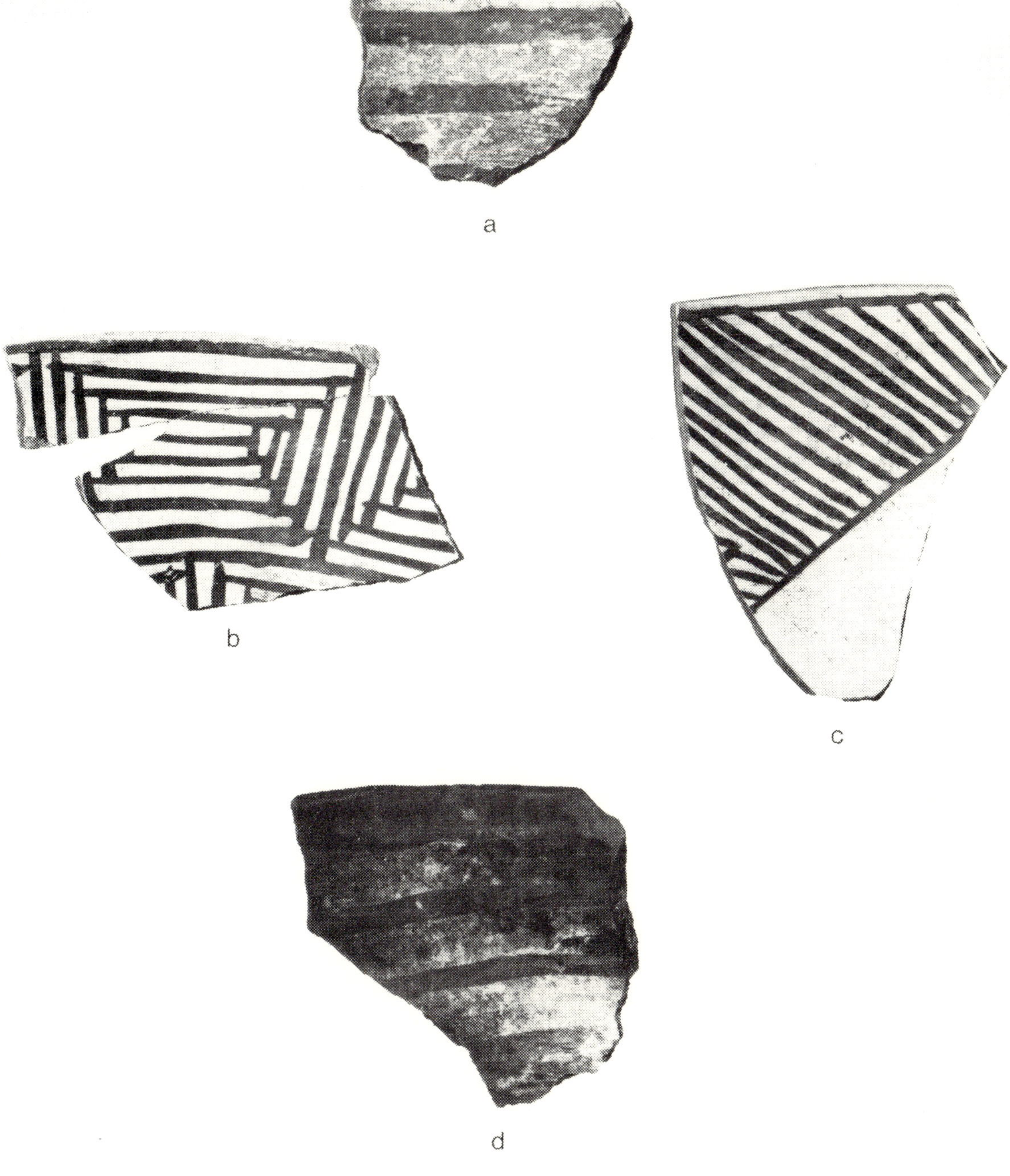

Figure 3.8 Tusayan White Wares. a, Sosi Black-on-white, b, Flagstaff Black-on-white; c, Dogoszhi Black-on-white; d, Black Mesa Black-on-white (length of c is 9.5 cm).

14 bowl forms. One sherd of each form was a rim, while the remaining 14 sherds were body sherds. The subtype Black Mesa/Sosi Black-on-white was implemented for those sherds too small to place in either Black Mesa Black-on-white or Sosi Black-on-white. They generally exhibited a wide line, but no other design elements were present that would distinguish one type from the others. Eighteen sherds (0.26 percent) comprised this sample. Four sherds represented jar forms and 14 sherds represented bowl forms. There were no jar rim sherds; seven sherds were bowl rims. Sosi Black-on-white (Fig. 3.8a) was represented by only seven sherds (0.10 percent), all of which were bowl forms: one rim sherd and six body sherds.

Dogoszhi Black-on-white (Fig. 3.8c) was represented by three sherds (0.04 percent). Jar forms were represented by one body sherd. Bowl forms were represented by one rim sherd and one body sherd. All seven sherds (0.10 percent) of Flagstaff Black-on-white (Fig. 3.8b) were bowl forms. They consisted of three rim sherds and four body sherds. Five bowl sherds (0.07 percent) represented Shato Black-on-white: one rim sherd and four body sherds.

There were 48 sherds (0.69 percent) that could not be assigned to a specific type. However, their paste, surface treatment, tempering materials, and paint, indicated that the sherds were Tusayan White Wares. This sample consisted of 20 jar forms, of which 2 were rim sherds and 18 were body sherds, and 29 bowl forms, of which 1 was a rim sherd and 27 were body sherds.

Tusayan Gray Wares

A total of 61 Tusayan Gray Wares, or 0.87 percent of the sample, was recovered (Table 3.2). Two types were recognized. A single bowl body sherd (0.01 percent) of Medicine Gray was recovered, and 60 jar sherds (0.86 percent) were Tusayan Corrugated, of which 8 were rim sherds and 52 were body sherds.

Little Colorado White Wares

Three different types of Little Colorado White Wares were identified (n=33, 0.47 percent; Table 3.3; Fig. 3.9). Holbrook Black-on-white (Black Mesa style; Fig. 3.9d), generally referred to as Holbrook A, is represented by a single bowl rim sherd (0.01 percent). Holbrook Black-on-white (Sosi style; Fig. 3.9e), generally referred to as Holbrook B, is represented by 11 sherds (0.16 percent): one jar body sherd, two bowl rim sherds, and eight bowl body sherds. Only six sherds (0.09 percent) of Padre Black-on-white were recovered: three jar rim sherds and three bowl rim sherds.

Fifteen sherds (0.21 percent) that could not be assigned to a specific pottery type were classified as unidentified Little Colorado White Wares. This group included 3 jar body sherds and 12 bowl body sherds.

Table 3.3

CERAMIC TYPES (SHERDS) FROM TOWNSEND-DIVIDE (AZ I:10:30, ASM)

Little Colorado White Wares and Tsegi Orange Wares

Provenience	Holbrook B/W (Black Mesa Style) J	Holbrook B/W (Black Mesa Style) B	Holbrook B/W (Sosi Style) J	Holbrook B/W (Sosi Style) B	Padre B/W J	Padre B/W B	Unidentified Little Colorado White Ware J	Unidentified Little Colorado White Ware B	Medicine B/R J	Medicine B/R B	Tusayan B/R J	Tusayan B/R B	Kiet Siel B/R J	Kiet Siel B/R B	Cameron Polychrome J	Cameron Polychrome B	Unidentified Tsegi Orange Ware J	Unidentified Tsegi Orange Ware B
Feature 1																		
Fill [S1]	0	0	0	1/2	0	2/1	0	0/5	0	10/9	0	2/5	0	0	0	1/0	0/6	2/14
Floor [S20]	0	0	0/1	0	0	0	0/1	0	0	0	0	0	0	0	0	0	0	0
Feature 1.1	0	0	0	0	0	0	0	0	0	0	0	0	0	0	0	0	0	0
Feature 1.2	0	0	0	0	0	0	0	0	0	0	0	0	0	0	0	0	0	0
Feature 1.28	0	0	0	0	0	0	0	0	0	0	0	0	0	0	0	0	0	0
Feature 1.29	0	0	0	0	0	0	0	0	0	0	0	0	0	0	0	0	0	0
Feature 1.30	0	0	0	0	0	0	0	0	0	0	0	0	0	0	0	0	0	0
Feature 2	0	0	0	0	0	0	0	0	0	0	0	0	0	0	0	0	0	0
Feature 3	0	0	0	0	0	0	0	0	0	0	0	0	0	0	0	0	0	0
Feature 5																		
Fill [S1]	0	1/0	0	1/6	0	1/2	0/2	0/7	0	1/2	0	5/5	0	1/0	1/0	0/1	2/2	0/12
Floor [S20]	0	0	0	0	0	0	0	0	0	0	0	0	0	0	0	0	0	0
Fill[S2]	0	0	0	0	0	0	0	0	0	0	0	0	0	0	0	0	0/2	0
Floor [S21]	0	0	0	0	0	0	0	0	0	0	0	0	0	0	0	0	0	0
Feature 5.1	0	0	0	0	0	0	0	0	0	0	0	0	0	0	0	0	0	0
Feature 5.3	0	0	0	0	0	0	0	0	0	0	0	0	0	0	0	0	0	0
Feature 5.4	0	0	0	0	0	0	0	0	0	0	0	0	0	0	0	0	0	0
Feature 5.5	0	0	0	0	0	0	0	0	0	0	0	0	0	0	0	0	0	0
Feature 5.6	0	0	0	0	0	0	0	0	0	0	0	0	0	0	0	0	0	0
Feature 5.9	0	0	0	0	0	0	0	0	0	0	0	0	0	0	0	0	0	0
Feature 6	0	0	0	0	0	0	0	0	0	0	0	0	0	0	0	0	0	0
Feature 7	0	0	0	0	0	0	0	0	0	0	0	0	0	0	0	0	0	0
Trench 1	0	0	0	0	0	0	0	0	0	0	0	0	0	0	0	0	0/1	0
Trench 2	0	0	0	0	0	0	0	0	0	0	0	0	0	0	0	0	0/1	0
Subtotal	0	1/0	0/1	2/8	0/0	3/3	0/3	0/12	0	12/11	0	9/10	0	1/0	1/0	1/1	2/12	2/26
Total	1		11		6		15		23		19		1		3		42	

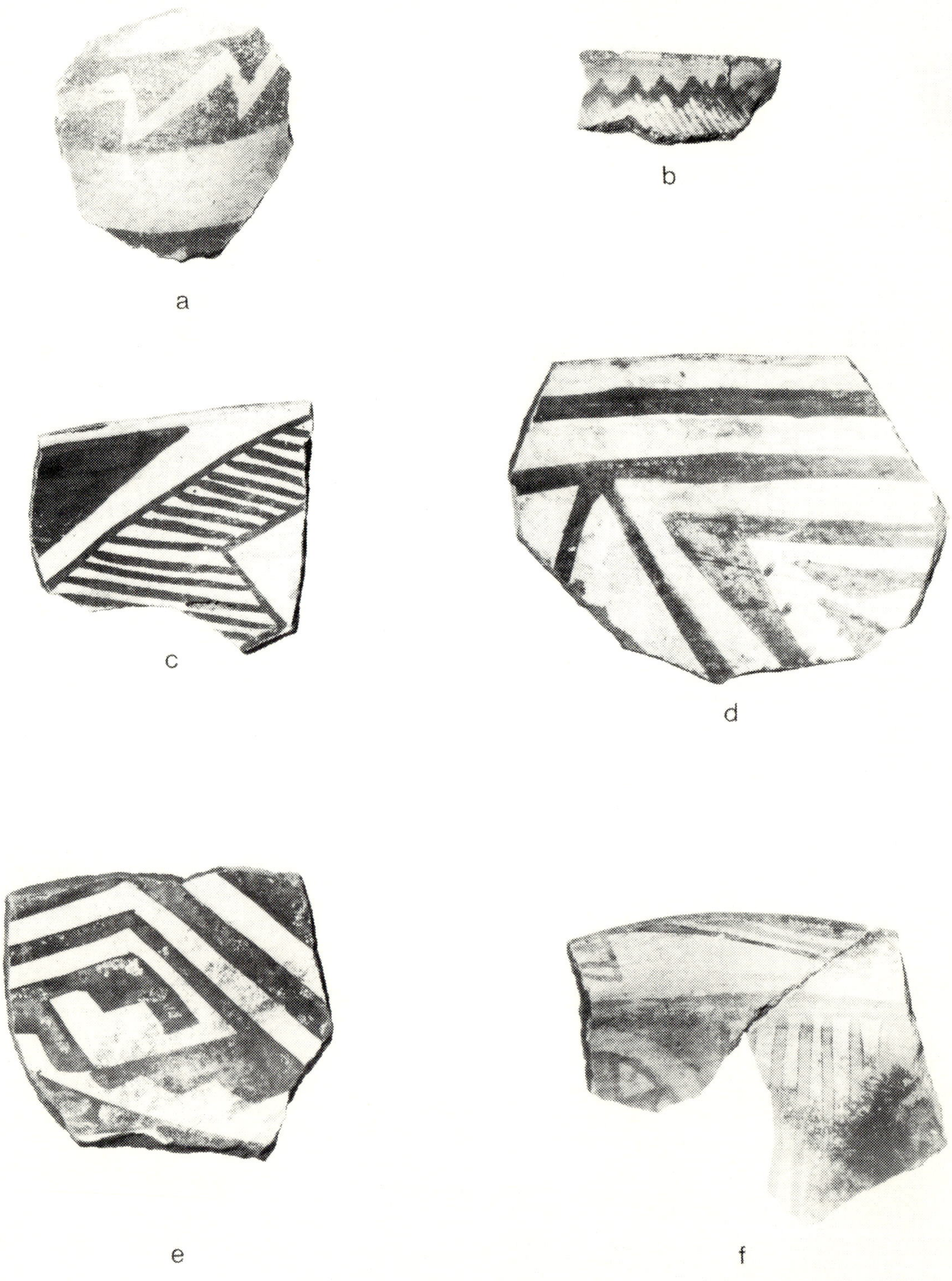

Figure 3.9 Little Colorado White Wares and miscellaneous types. a, Cibola White Ware (Puerco Black-on-white?); b, Sacaton Red-on-Buff; c, Tusayan White ware with mineral paint; d, Holbrook (A) Black-on-white; e, Holbrook (B) Black-on-white; f, Black Mesa Black-on-white on Flagstaff bowl form (width of d is 10.9 cm).

Tsegi Orange Wares

A total of 88 sherds (1.26 percent) was classified as Tsegi Orange Wares, with four types recognized (Table 3.3; Fig. 3.10).

Medicine Black-on-red (Fig. 3.10d) was represented by 23 bowl sherds (0.33 percent), of which 12 were rim sherds and 11 were body sherds. Tusayan Black-on-red (Fig. 3.10a-b) was represented by 19 bowl sherds (0.27 percent); 9 were rim sherds and 10 were body sherds. A single bowl rim sherd (0.9 percent) of Kiet Siel Black-on-red (?) was represented. Three sherds (0.04 percent) of Cameron Polycrome (Fig. 3.10c) were recovered, including one jar rim, one bowl rim, and one bowl body sherd.

There were 42 Tsegi Orange Ware sherds (0.60 percent) that could not be assigned to a specific type. This group included 2 jar rim sherds, 12 jar body sherds, 2 bowl rim sherds, and 26 bowl body sherds.

San Francisco Mountain Gray Wares

A total of 88 (0.97 percent) San Francisco Mountain Gray Wares was recovered, with 3 types identified (Table 3.4). Deadman's Gray was represented by 28 sherds (0.40 percent) of which 1 was a jar rim sherd, 13 were jar body sherds, and 14 were bowl body sherds. Deadman's Black-on-gray consisted of a scant two bowl sherds (0.03 percent); one was a rim sherd and the other a body sherd. The subsample of Deadman's Fugitive Red was comprised of 38 sherds (0.54 percent). Sixteen were jar body sherds and 22 were bowl body sherds.

Other Wares and Types

Four pottery types were identified that did not fall under the pottery types mentioned above (Table 3.4; Fig. 3.9). A single jar rim sherd (0.01 percent) of Sacaton Red-on-buff (Fig. 3.9b) was recovered from Townsend-Divide. Wingfield Plain, from the northern periphery of the Hohokam, was represented by 87 sherds (1.24 percent). Of these, 13 were jar body sherds, 21 were bowl rim sherds, and 53 were bowl body sherds. One partially reconstructable bowl was found in the fill of Feature 5, a pit house. Six sherds (0.09 percent) of Prescott Gray Ware, probably Prescott Gray, were recovered from Townsend-Divide. This group included two jar rim sherds, three jar body sherds, and one bowl rim sherd. A scant three (0.04 percent) sherds were unidentifiable Cibola White Wares (Fig. 3.9a): one jar rim sherd and two jar body sherds.

Discussion

The analysis of the Alameda Brown Wares recovered from excavations at Townsend-Divide indicates a Sinagua occupation of the site during late Rio de Flag, Angell-Winona times (A.D. 1000-1100). The

Figure 3.10 Tsegi Orange Wares. a-b, Tusayan Black-on-Red; c, Cameron Polychrome; d, Medicine Black-on-red (width of d is 15.5 cm).

Table 3.4

CERAMIC TYPES (SHERDS FROM TOWNSEND-DIVIDE (AZ I:10:30, ASM)

San Francisco Mountain Gray Wares and Other Types

Provenience	Deadmans Gray J	Deadmans Gray B	Deadmans B/G J	Deadmans B/G B	Deadmans Fugitive Red J	Deadmans Fugitive Red B	Sacaton R/Bf J	Sacaton R/Bf B	Wingfield Plain J	Wingfield Plain B	Prescott Gray Ware J	Prescott Gray Ware B	Unidentified Cibola White Ware J	Unidentified Cibola White Ware B
Feature 1														
Fill [S1]	1/3	0/6	0	1/0	0/9	0/14	1/0	0	0/8	6/23	1/1	0	1/1	0
Floor [S20]	0	0	0	0	0	0	0	0	0	3/11	0	0	0	0
Feature 1.1	0	0	0	0	0	0	0	0	0	0	0	0	0	0
Feature 1.2	0	0	0	0	0	0	0	0	0	0	0	0	0	0
Feature 1.28	0	0	0	0	0	0	0	0	0	0	0	0	0	0
Feature 1.29	0	0	0	0	0	0	0	0	0	0	0	0	0	0
Feature 1.30	0	0	0	0	0	0	0	0	0	0	0	0	0	0
Feature 2	0	0	0	0	0	0	0	0	0	0	0	0	0	0
Feature 3	0/1	0	0	0/1	0/1	0	0	0	0	2/2	0	0	0/1	0
Feature 5														
Fill [S1]	0/8	0/7	0	0	0/4	0/8	0	0	0/3	9/17	1/2	0	0	0
Floor [S20]	0	0	0	0	0	0	0	0	0	0	0	0	0	0
Fill [S2]	0	0	0	0	0/1	0	0	0	0	0	0	0	0	0
Floor [S21]	0	0	0	0	0	0	0	0	0	0	0	0	0	0
Feature 5.1	0	0	0	0	0	0	0	0	0	0	0	0	0	0
Feature 5.3	0	0	0	0	0	0	0	0	0	0	0	0	0	0
Feature 5.4	0	0/1	0	0	0	0	0	0	0	0	0	0	0	0
Feature 5.5	0/1	0	0	0	0	0	0	0	0	0	0	0	0	0
Feature 5.6	0	0	0	0	0	0	0	0	0	0	0	0	0	0
Feature 5.9	0	0	0	0	0	0	0	0	0	0	0	0	0	0
Feature 6	0	0	0	0	0	0	0	0	0	0	0	0	0	0
Feature 7	0	0	0	0	0/1	0	0	0	0/2	0	0	0	0	0
Trench 1	0	0	0	0	0	0	0	0	0	0	0	0	0	0
Trench 2	0	0	0	0	0	0	0	0	0	0	0	1/0	0	0
Subtotal	1/13	0/14	0	1/1	0/16	0/22	1/0	0	0/13	21/53	2/3	1/0	1/2	0
TOTAL	28		2		38		1		87		6		3	

predominance of Late Angell Brown suggests a more intensive use of the site toward the latter part of that time. Decorated wares analyzed during the Alameda Brown Ware study also confirm this date (Fig. 3.11).

The objectives of the early and late Angell Brown analysis were twofold:

1. To further refine the A.D. 1000 to 1100 time period in the Sinagua area through an analysis of temper distinctions in Angell Brown, and;

2. To lend supporting evidence for an early Preeruptive Hohokam presence in the area through association of Hohokam pottery with Rio de Flag Brown and early Angell Brown.

Unfortunately, the temporal distinctions between early and late Angell Brown, as anticipated, were not readily apparent. It was predicted that with increasing depth, the proportions of early versus late Angell Brown would become more dissimilar. Thus, in theory, a stratigraphic column would reveal a decrease in late Angell (and associated decorated wares dating from around A.D. 1066 to 1100 and an increase in Rio de Flag phase (A.D. 1000-1065) ceramics including more Rio de Flag Brown and early Angell Brown. No pattern was recognized, however, when frequencies of early and late were plotted against increased depth.

While several explanations are probably necessary, one appears obvious. Given the nature of modern disturbance in the area (including a large ponderosa pine tree on the site), and the depositional history of the area, it is possible that most of the materials lost their primary context with repeated churning and redeposition. The lack of both valid natural and cultural strata preclude any elaborate discussion on context. However, brief mention is made regarding artifacts located on the floors of houses.

The strongest evidence for original context is within Feature 1. The occurrence of Wingfield Plain in a pit house with a peripheral posthole pattern reminiscent of Hohokam pit house is an interesting phenomenon. Wingfield Plain, a Hohokam utility ware characteristically tempered with a very coarse crushed mica schist, is usually found in more southern assemblages. Although occasionally found in the Flagstaff area, its presence is generally confined to the period after A.D. 1066. Historically, the occurrence of Hohokam-like ceramics, figurines, trash mounds, and the like, is synonymous with the Hohokam in the northland. Dating of Wingfield Plain is estimated at about A.D. 1100 (Colton 1941a: 46), or A.D. 700 through about A.D. 1450 (Breternitz 1966: 31).

Hohokam-style houses, documented in the area, usually date to the Winona phase, around A.D. 1070 to 1100. These dates are derived from both ceramic and tree-ring dates for such sites as NA 2133A (Colton 1946: 185-186) and NA 2098A (McGregor 1941: 290-291). Colton (1946: 270), in fact, viewed the Winona phase as a time during which the Hohokam settled near Winona, east of Flagstaff. Pilles (1979: 471),

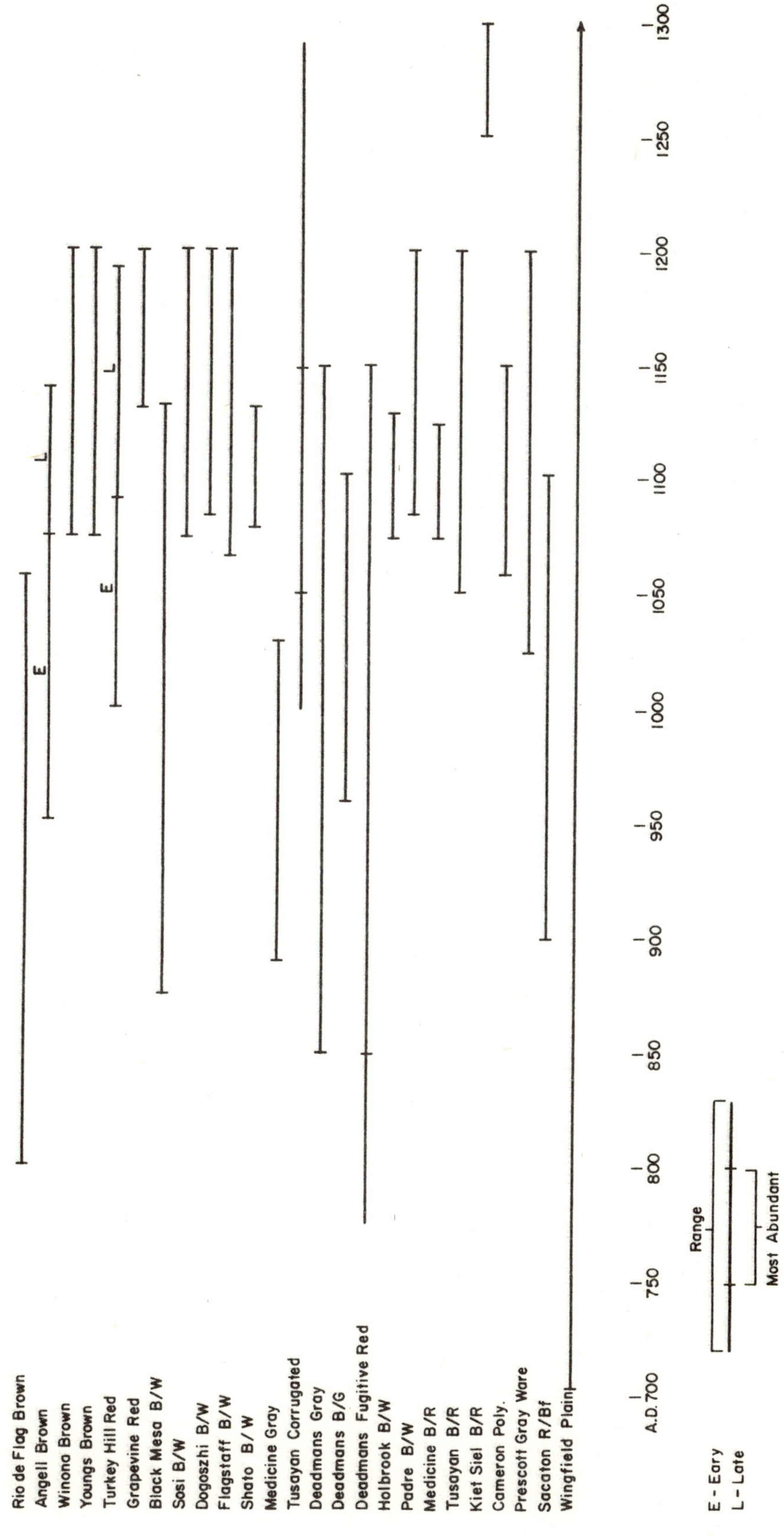

Figure 3.11. Temporal distribution of ceramic types from Townsend-Divide.

though, argues for a Preeruptive Hohokam presence based on Hohokam-like cultural goods and the unusual pit house styles in early Sinagua sites.

Pit structures at the Jack Smith Alcove Pit House Site (NA 1298B), were assigned a Sinagua affiliation but contained Hohokam-like post patterns and dated to Angell-Winona-Padre phases (around A.D. 1050-1100). It is interesting to note that this pit house style is common to neither Sinagua period (Colton 1946: 104).

Based on the plain ware analysis, the information relating to the two above-mentioned points is inconclusive. The absence of good natural or cultural strata (or both), which are necessary for relative dating, made fine-tuned dating attempts almost impossible. An evaluation of early/late Angell Brown frequencies in association with their decorated Kayenta counterparts might reflect slight temporal changes not recognized elsewhere in the area. If expanded, this information would prove useful in discerning possible functional differences on both an intrasite level and a site-specific level. A more exhaustive brown ware analysis would also answer questions regarding functional differences between sites with a predominance of early (as opposed to late) Angell Brown, as well as questions about the early/late distinction being reflected in vessel form.

Few early ceramic analyses based on excavated materials lend themselves to such comparisons. Most studies provide gross ware and type counts with little concern for temper anomalies or smudged varieties. None, with one possible exception, attempts to subdivide on the basis of temper distinctions, as in this study (see Pilles [1969: 98]).

Although analysis expectations exceeded results, useful information was obtained regarding Hohokam contact in the area. The results suggest Hohokam influence in the Sinagua area as early as A.D. 1000. The occurrence of Rio de Flag and early Angell Brown at considerable depths, in association with Wingfield Plain in a fairly reliable context, demonstrates Hohokam influence in the area, not necessarily as a group but perhaps as individual traders (see Fish and others [1980]). Conversely, it may well be that the Sinagua were in the Hohokam area and returned with ceramics as trade items.

Additional excavation data, with a more rigorous focus on analysis of local ceramics, especially typological distinctions, may better define the Sinagua and their place in Southwest prehistory.

The nonlocally produced decorated ceramics (Fig. 3.11), tend to support the occupation span noted above. Specifically, traditionally defined pottery types coincide with the date ranges of the Alameda Brown Wares. Black Mesa Black-on-white (n=16, 0.23 percent) is best dated between A.D 875 to 1130 (Breternitz 1966) as a trade ware. Tusayan Corrugated (n=60, 0.86 percent) is most abundant between A.D. 1050 to 1150. Breternitz (1966: 85) offers a range of A.D. 1075 to 1125 for Medicine Black-on-red (n=23, 0.33 percent). Similarly, Tusayan Black-on-red dates from about A.D. 1050 to 1150 as a trade product (Breternitz 1966: 99).

The decorated black-on-white ceramics (140 sherds, or 2 percent of the ceramic assemblage) from Townsend-Divide are enigmatic in some respects. Although by no means abundant, there are a few sherds that are worth mentioning, as they exhibit an admixture of technological and stylistic attributes of traditionally defined Southwestern pottery types. For example, one sherd (Fig. 3.9c) has evidence of a mineral paint applied in an organic medium. The paint is not well controlled, thus evidencing the underlying organic medium. In some aspects of technology, it appears to be a Tusayan White Ware (polished with sand temper), although the mineral paint suggests affinities with Cibola White Wares. Stylistically, the designs reflect elements of both Sosi Black-on-white and Dogoszhi Black-on-white. A. J. Lindsay, Jr. (ASM) has suggested that it is not a Tusayan White Ware, but rather that it has affinities with the Puerco series of Cibola White Wares. Perhaps it belongs to one of the five ceramic groups--PSM (Polished, Sand temper, Mineral paint)--within the Cibola White Wares as defined by Hantman and others (1984: 21). There is another sherd (Fig. 3.9f) that exhibits a Black Mesa Black-on-white stylistic design on a Flagstaff Black-on-white bowl form (flared rim).

Because the sample from Townsend-Divide is extremely small, the observations given above are qualitative at best. Peter Pilles, of the Coconino National Forest, has indicated to us that it is not unusual for black-on-white ceramics in the Flagstaff area to exhibit various combinations of stylistic and technological attributes that appear to vary independently. Traditional pottery types mask this variability.

This comment suggests an important and productive research area for ceramics in northern Arizona. Specifically, it implies that stylistic and technological variability exists within, and cuts across, traditionally defined wares such as Tusayan White Ware, Little Colorado White Ware, and Cibola White Ware, which are the predominant decorated ceramics found on Sinagua sites. Reid (1984) thoroughly discusses this kind of variability in Cibola White Wares. Ceramic analyses that focus on the provenience or regional distribution of ceramic style and ceramic technology in the Flagstaff area may yield important information regarding centers of production and the means of trade and exchange (see, for example, Hantman and others [1984] for a discussion of this problem). It is clear that pottery was coming into the Sinagua from the north, northeast, and east, but by what mechanisms remains unclear (see Fish and others 1980).

Flaked Stone

A total of 345 flaked stone artifacts was recovered from Townsend-Divide, including 305 flakes or flake fragments and 40 retouched pieces. All of the flaked stone was recovered from four well defined features excavated at the site. For the analysis of these artifacts, a number of metric and nonmetric attributes were recorded to determine the preferred lithic material types used by the inhabitants, the types of stone working operations done at the site (such as raw material procurement, tool manufacture, and tool modification), and the tasks the tools were designed to perform. To determine these factors, the assemblage was broken down into lithic debris and retouched pieces for further analysis. The analysis technique follows closely a format developed previously for use on projects such as this with small flaked stone assemblages (Tagg and Huckell 1984). This method of analysis was patterned after a more detailed analysis format used by Rozen (1981) to interpret the various steps of tool manufacture from primary (core reduction) through secondary (tool manufacture and remodification).

Debitage

This category includes unmodified flaked stone artifacts such as complete and fragmentary flakes and shatter.

Methods

Several metric and nonmetric variables were recorded for each artifact: artifact type, maximum dimension, raw material type, amount of cortex, striking platform type, and lipping. From these variables, a description of the types of reduction activities occuring at the site can be attempted.

The artifact types consists of complete and fragmentary flakes, and shatter. Complete flakes are all flakes in which the striking platform, and both the lateral and distal edges are intact. Fragmentary flakes are further subdivided into those with platforms and those without platforms. Fragments with platforms are proximal flake fragments which retain all or most of the striking platform, but have lost the distal end of the flake through breakage. Fragments without platforms are those distal and medial fragments that are missing the striking platform and portions of the lateral or distal ends as a result of breakage. Shatter includes irregular, angular pieces of debris in which the interior and exterior surfaces cannot be distinguished.

The maximum dimension was recorded on each piece of debitage using a metric size class chart created by Huckell (1984: 96), which consists of a series of arbitrarily numbered square units drawn on graph paper (Fig. 3.12). Raw material type, and the presence or absence of cortex on the exterior surface of the piece, was recorded for all debitage. On those flakes or flake fragments with striking platforms, the platform type was recorded using four categories: cortical platforms, which are entirely or partially covered with cortex; plain platforms, which are plain, noncortical surfaces with no flake scars; faceted platforms are plain, noncortical surfaces with portions of two or more flake scars running across their surface; and crushed platforms, which are those whose type cannot by determined since the platform was destroyed by crushing or shattering during the removal of the flake.

The final attribute recorded on those complete or fragmentary flakes with platforms was the presence or absence of lipping. "Lipping"

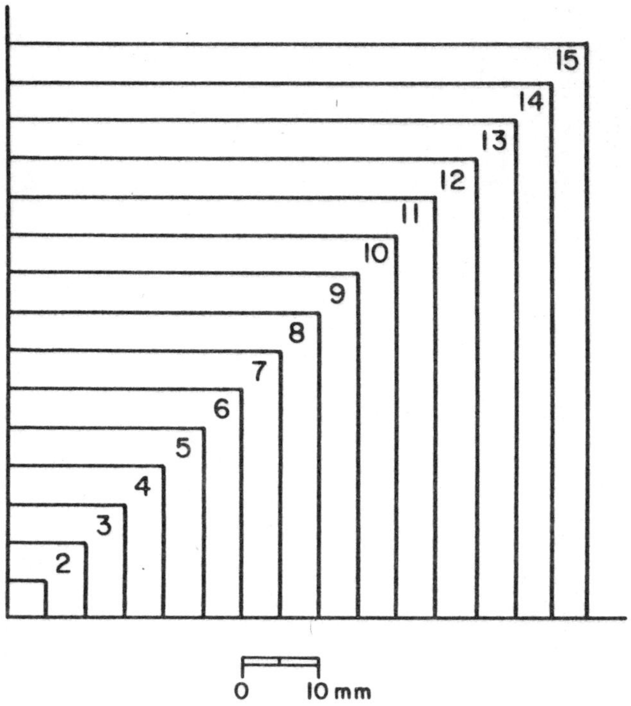

Figure 3.12 Size class chart for debitage measurements.

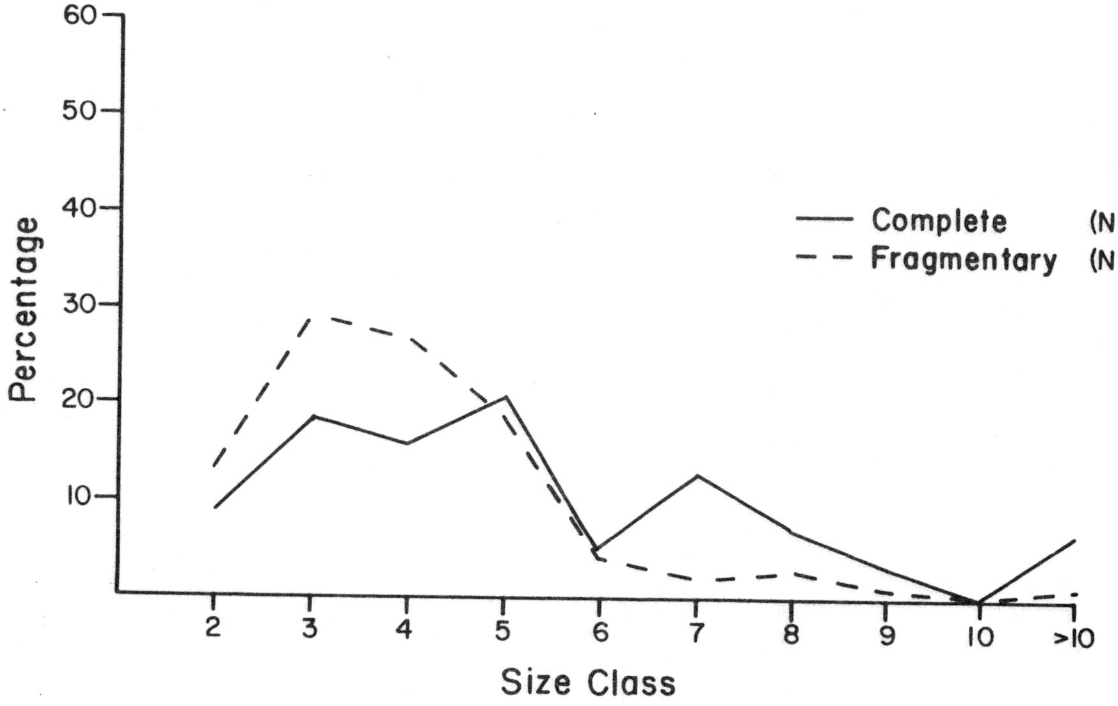

Figure 3.13 Percentage of debitage per size class.

is the term given to a protruding lip or overhang on the interior edge of the striking platform of a flake produced from the sharp angle the flake is removed by, and is generally associated with soft hammer bifacial retouching of an implement. Although it is not always visible to the eye, running a fingernail over the interior edge of the platform and detecting resistance will indicate its presence.

Results

Tables 3.5 and 3.6 present the results of the debitage analysis. As illustrated, flake fragments dominate the assemblage with 65.2 percent of the sample, or 199 artifacts (including fragments with and without platforms and shatter). There is also a relatively high percentage of complete flakes, with 106 specimens, or 34.8 percent of the sample. The size of the debitage trends towards the smaller end of the spectrum, as is clearly illustrated in Figure 3.13. It can be seen that although the graphs for both samples are quite similar, more than 70 percent of both groups are less than size 6 (3 mm) in maximum dimension, there are some obvious and expected differences. Complete flakes tend to be larger (the curve peaks at size 5), and flake fragments tend to be smaller (the curve peaks at size 3).

The raw material types used by the inhabitants of Townsend-Divide consist almost entirely of coarse-grained materials. Ten raw material types were used, with chert, basalt, and obsidian apparently the preferred materials (Table 3.6). Chert was the most commonly utilized material, making up 45.6 percent (139 pieces) of the sample. Unlike the very fine-grained cryptocrystalline texture commonly associated with chert, the material at Townsend-Divide is more coarse-grained, being more closely related in texture to quartzite; it would not be too out of line to call the material quartzitic chert. Only a few fine-grained chert flakes are present in the assemblage. Basalt is also very common, making up 42.3 percent of the sample (129 specimens), and obsidian is the third most common material comprising 7.2 percent of the sample (22 artifacts). These three raw materials are all locally available; chert from the Paleozoic exposures in and around the San Francisco Peaks, basalt from the numerous lava beds in the region, and obsidian in great quantities on and around Government Mountain, approximately 25 miles to the west. The remainder of the assemblage, less than 5 percent, is made up of small quantities of chalcedony, quartzite, rhyolite, jasper, agate, limestone, and quartz.

Cortex is generally lacking on the debitage from the site, with 87.2 percent of the assemblage lacking it completely. This holds true for the platform types also, with 65.3 percent (109 specimens) having plain platforms. Crushed platforms are also common, with 34 present, or 20.4 percent of the sample. Less than 10 percent of the assemblage exhibits cortical or faceted platforms.

Table 3.5

DEBITAGE VARIABLES

					Fea. 5		
	N	%	Fea. 1 [S1]	Fea. 3 [S1]	S1	S2	Fea. 7 [S1]
ARTIFACT TYPE	305						
Complete	106	34.8	50	2	47	6	1
Fragment + platform	61	20.0	39	1	18	3	
Fragment – platform	112	36.7	64	3	37	8	
Shatter	26	8.5	11		13	2	
Fragment Size	199						
2	26	13.1	17	2	6	1	
3	58	29.1	36		20	2	
4	57	28.6	32		20	5	
5	36	18.1	14	1	16	5	
6	8	4.0	6	1	1		
7	5	2.5	3		2		
8	6	3.0			1		
9	1	.5					
10	2	1.0	2				
Complete Size	106						
2	10	9.4	4		5	1	
3	20	18.9	9	2	5	4	
4	17	16.0	10		7		
5	23	21.7	8		15		
6	5	4.7	3		1	1	
7	13	12.3	6		6		1
8	8	7.5	3		5		
9	4	3.8	3		1		
>10	8	7.5	4		4		
Cortex	305						
Present	39	12.8	17		19	3	
Absent	266	87.2	147	6	96	16	1
Platform Type	167						
Cortical	7	4.2	5		2		
Plain	109	65.2	58	1	46	4	
Faceted	17	10.2	8		7	2	
Crushed	34	20.4	18	2	10	3	1
Lipping	167						
Present	18	10.9	8	1	7	2	
Absent	149	89.1	81	8	58	7	1

Table 3.6

DEBITAGE RAW MATERIAL TYPES

	N	%	Fea. 1 (S1)	Fea. 3 (S1)	Fea. 5 S1	Fea. 5 S2	Fea. 7 (S1)
Chert	139	45.6	79		47	13	
Chalcedony	5	1.6	1		2	2	
Jasper	1	0.3			1		
Agate	1	0.3	1				
Quartzite	4	1.3	2		2		
Basalt	129	42.3	69	5	51	3	1
Rhyolite	2	0.7			2		
Limestone	1	0.3	1				
Obsidian	22	7.2	11	1	9	1	
Quartz	1	0.3			1		
TOTAL	305		164	6	115	19	1

Retouched Pieces

Retouched pieces are defined as pieces of flaked stone exhibiting evidence of secondary retouch, with flakes removed from one or more edges, usually in a uniform fashion (Tagg and Huckell 1984: 76).

Methods

The retouched pieces recovered from Townsend-Divide are classified into one of eight artifact types based on morphology similar to traditionally defined tool types commonly used in the Southwest. These type names do not necessarily suggest functional pieces, since no studies of use wear were conducted to indicate how, or if, the artifact had been utilized as a tool. In some cases, pieces were further divided within a category to distinguish variation within the specific artifact types. Depending on the artifact type, a number of metric and nonmetric attributes were recorded on each retouched piece, including material type, completeness, metric dimensions or size class, and edge damage or use wear. The seven artifact types are defined below, with definitions based on Rozen (1981).

Projectile points are small bifaces (20 mm to 60 mm long), usually trangular or lanceolate in shape, with some specialization in form to facilitate hafting, such as stems or notches.

Scrapers are unifacially retouched pieces that have a series of flakes removed from a flat surface along one or more margins of the interior of a flake, to create a fairly steep working angle and edge.

Unifaces are pieces exhibiting retouch along one margin, which are generally smaller, thinner, and exhibit more variability and less uniformity in edge shape than scrapers. This category includes unifacially retouched fragments too small to place in other categories.

Bifaces are those pieces exhibiting continuous bifacial flake removal from a common, continuous margin. They rarely exhibit evidence of pressure flaking, and have no specializations for hafting.

Spokeshaves are unifacially retouched pieces with a series of small flakes removed to create a concavity on one margin of a flake.

Perforators are those artifacts exhibiting projections or bits produced by unifacial or bifacial retouch, including drills. A drill has a pronounced bit, usually produced by bifacial retouch and exhibiting uniform and overlapping flake scars.

Cobble tools are natural river cobbles with one or more edges modified by intentional retouch or through use. Four subtypes were defined based on the type of retouch or use wear. Hammerstones exhibit battered margins from use as hammers to remove flakes from cores, and other battering tasks. Choppers have one edge of the cobble modified by flake removal to create an edge for cutting. Core-hammerstones are pieces which have had flakes removed from one or more margins, and which also exhibit battering from use as a hammer. Hammer-handstones exhibit battered margins from use as hammers, as well as worn facets on one or more surfaces from use as a grinding implement.

Cores are pieces of lithic material which have had large flakes removed for secondary use, and exhibit negative bulbs of percussion. Nonglobular pieces with two or more flakes removed to test the material were also included in this category.

Results

A total of 40 retouched pieces was recovered from the features at Townsend-Divide, comprising 11.7 percent of the flaked stone assemblage (Table 3.7).

Table 3.7

DISTRIBUTION OF RETOUCHED PIECES

	N	Fea. 1	Fea. 3	Fea. 5
Projectile points	10	8		2
Scrapers	1	1		
Unifaces	5		2	3
Bifaces	2	1		1
Spokeshaves	1	2		
Perforators	1			1
Cobble tools				
Core/hammer	1	1		
Hammer/handstone	1			1
Hammerstone	4	2		2
Chopper	1	1		
Cores				
Core	11	3	1	7
Tested cobble	3	3		

Projectile points represent the only culturally or temporally diagnostic artifacts present, with a total of 10 recovered (29.3 percent of the sample). Three separate styles of points are identified, as well as what are considered unfinished products (Fig. 3.14). All the recovered points are obsidian.

The most common style is a long, narrow, serrated point that is roughly triangular in shape (Fig. 3.14*d*-*h*). Five points of this style were recovered (three from Feature 1 and two from Feature 5) and

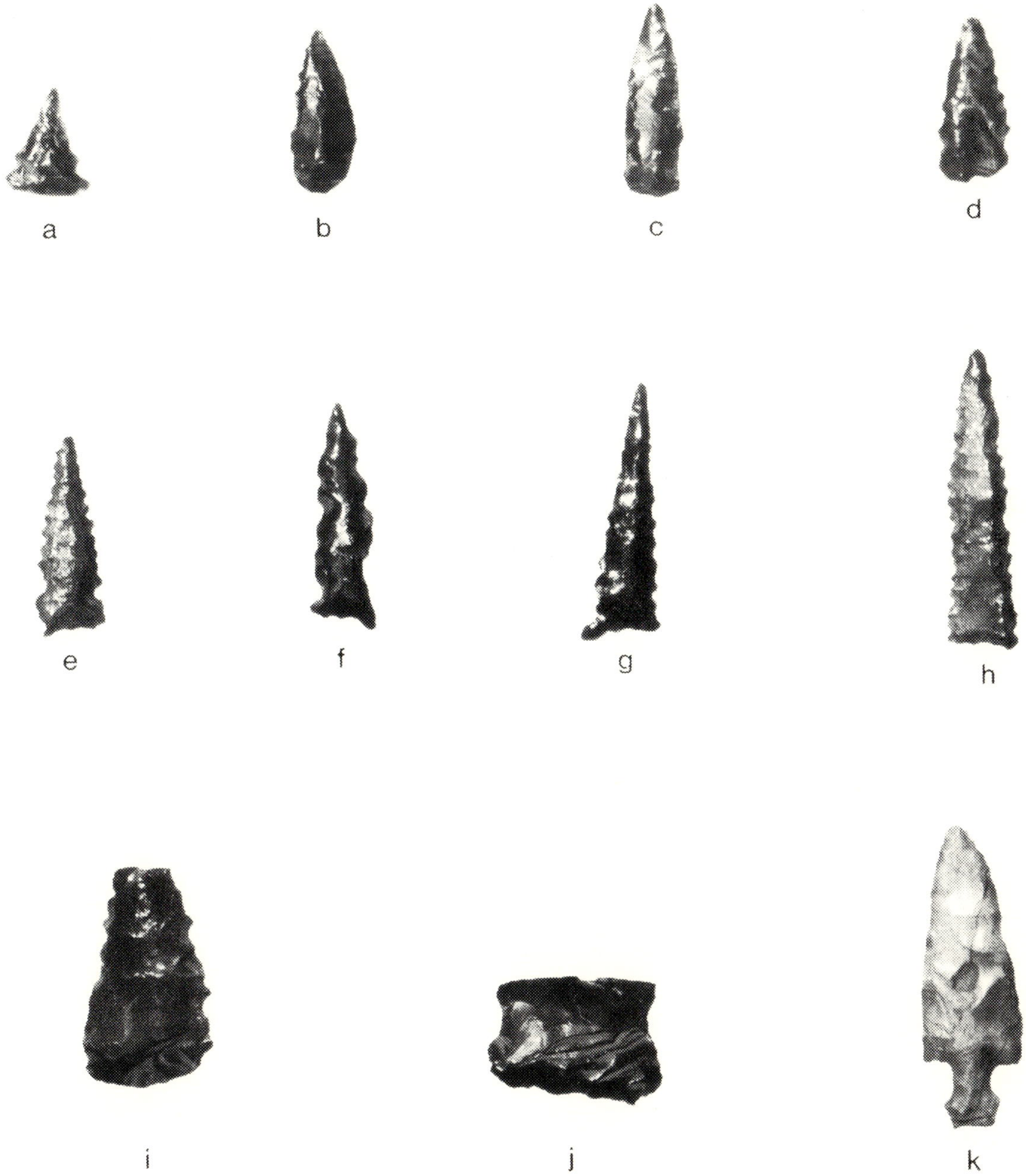

Figure 3.14 Projectile points from Townsend-Divide. a-j, obsidian; k, chert (length of k is 4.4 cm).

although they vary in length and base style, they clearly represent variations of the same style. They were all produced by pressure flaking, with flake scars obliterating the original flake surface. Four of the specimens are finely flaked and thin (Fig. 3.14d-e, g-h), while the fifth is thick and irregular (Fig. 3.14f). They range in size from 2.9 cm to 4.9 cm long, 0.7 cm to 1.4 cm wide, and 0.3 cm to 1.0 cm thick. The basal form of the points vary; two have small tangs and a concave base; one has a serrated base; and one has a slightly uneven, notched base. It has been suggested that the "notches" may in fact have been produced as part of the serrated edges, but still could have been used for hafting (Rondeau 1975: 12).

These serrated points fall under point styles O and P as suggested by McGregor (1941: 187-189, Fig. 64), whose point typology for the Sinagua is widely used. The style is most common in Angell-Winona-Padre and Elden phase sites, about A.D. 1066 to 1200. They are almost always made of obsidian, are serrated with low lateral notches, and have been compared to the serrated points typical of the Sacaton phase Hohokam (as illustrated by Gladwin and others [1937: Plate LXXXV]) and Cohonina (McGregor 1941). This would place them in the Pueblo II time period, which seems to be the agreed upon time frame for this point style (Bartlett 1934: 14-17; McGregor 1936: 32-33; McGregor 1941: 187-188; Rondeau 1975: 13).

In addition to the complete, well made serrated points, there are two crude specimens that appear to be unfinished products of this style (Fig. 3.14b-c). They exhibit poorly controlled flaking, very steep flake scars, and much of the surface of the original flake is still visible. Rondeau (1975: 14) suggests that these may be crudely finished points, or perhaps symbolic points such as are worn for decoration on ceremonial costumes of the Hopi.

The second point style is represented by a small triangular arrow point with a flat base (Fig. 3.14a). The point appears to be slightly serrated, with deep serrations near the base, and it is possible that it is a reworked example of the first point type. It resembles an example found at Snaketown that is illustrated with the Sacaton phase serrated points (Gladwin and others 1937: Plate LXXXVh). This is also a common projectile point style throughout Arizona

Also represented by one specimen is a medium-sized dart point fragment. Very little remains of the point other than the base, which has been reworked to a new form (Fig. 3.14j). The base appears to have come from a corner or side-notched point, but because the broken margin has been reworked so intensively, it cannot be identified more precisely. The artifact is in an unknown form, and it is unclear whether another point was being attempted; perhaps it was a gaming piece or ornament. Points of this size are generally associated with earlier, preceramic cultures, but have also been found in small numbers in Angell-Winona-Padre phase sites around Flagstaff (McGregor 1941: 191, Fig. 65).

The final point is another unfinished product of a style of a larger dart point. The artifact is finely flaked near the tip, which has been snapped off during manufacture, but appears incomplete in the basal region because much of the surface of the original flake remains intact (Fig. 3.14i).

A projectile point was also recovered from the surface of the site during the testing phase of the project (Sullivan 1980). It is a relatively complete side-notched point of chert (Fig. 3.14k). The long (4.5 cm), slender specimen is well flaked, with a long stem and what appears to have been a flat, T-shaped base (both ends of the base are broken). This point is very dissimilar in style to those obsidian points found in the features; it is more closely related to points of Basketmaker II style (as illustrated by Morris and Burgh [1954, Fig. 81, Fig. 106i]). It is possible that the point is not related to the occupation of Townsend-Divide; it may have been picked up from an earlier site and transported to Townsend-Divide later in time.

Unifaces are represented by five artifacts: four very small fragments and one complete specimen. The complete specimen, made of obsidian, is a small flake with flakes removed from one edge. Two of the fragments have one flat surface and steep edge angles and were probably scrapers. The remaining two fragments are very small, representing fragments with a small section of unifacial retouch on one margin. All the fragments are chert.

Two biface fragments were recovered, one from the fill of Feature 1 and one from the fill of Feature 5. Both artifacts are best described as preforms due to their unfinished appearance. Preforms are described as large, thick, crudely flaked artifacts that probably represent unfinished bifaces (Tagg and Huckell 1984: 85). One preform is a complete obsidian flake with finely flaked margins, but has much of the original surface of the flake remaining. The second preform is a large, crudely flaked basalt fragment with a few widely spaced flakes taken off bifacially.

One scraper was recovered from the fill of Feature 1. The chert specimen has a small piece broken off one side. The working edge was made with a series of large flakes removed from a flat surface on the flake, creating a slightly denticulate blade.

Also represented by one artifact is a basalt spokeshave. The fragment was recovered from the fill of Feature 1, and has a concavity created by the removal of a series of small, overlapping flakes.

One perforator was recovered from the fill of Feature 5. The chert artifact appears to have been a drill but the bit has been reworked or worn down to a very small projection, more like a graver. The bit has been produced with bifacial flake removal to isolate the projection from the flake.

A total of seven cobble tools was recovered, three from Feature 5 and four from Feature 1. Included in this category are four hammerstones and one each of core-hammerstones, hammer-handstones, and choppers. All the hammerstones are basalt cobbles, ranging in size from 6.7 cm to 9.4 cm long, 6.2 cm to 9.1 cm wide, and 5.1 cm to 6.0 cm thick, and weighing between 316 g and 762 g. All four specimens are well rounded: one specimen is heavily spalled with smooth margins from abrasion (Fig. 3.15a), while the remaining three have well rounded and shaped margins from long term or heavy use (Fig. 3.15b-d). The three well rounded specimens have red ochre stains on them: one has light stains over most of its surfaces, one has two distinct round stains on the rounded margin as well as a light stain on one face that has been smoothed from abrasion, and the last artifact has light stains on one face that has been pecked and worn smooth from abrasion. It seems apparent that these hammerstones were used for pigment grinding and other abrading tasks as well as for hammering.

The core-hammerstone is a chert core fragment that has battering, from use as a hammer, along the existing margin. The hammer-handstone is a complete quartzite cobble, 7.3 cm by 6.4 cm by 5.3 cm, that weighs 376 g. Two flat facets are worn by grinding, and battering is evident on both ends. The chopper is a fragment of a chert cobble that has had one margin bifacially flaked to produce an edge. Large flakes removed at a steep angle on one surface almost creates a scraperlike edge to the implement.

Cores represent the most abundant type of retouched piece in the assemblage. The assemblage includes eight cores--four from Feature 5, three from Feature 1, and one from Feature 3--and three tested cobbles from Feature 1. The cores are small exhausted pieces ranging from 3 cm to 6 cm in maximum dimension and weighing from 4 g to 151 g. All have multidirectional flake removal and exhibit little, if any, cortex. Four are chert, three are basalt, and one is obsidian. The tested cobbles are also small, ranging from 3 cm to 5 cm in maximum dimension and weighing from 14 g to 106 g. All are chert pieces with only a few flakes removed to test the suitability of the material for flake production.

Finally, a small quartz crystal from Feature 5 should be mentioned. The artifact is 2.1 cm long; although it has not been modified, it was clearly imported to the site, probably for decorative or ritual use.

Discussion

The flaked stone assemblage from Townsend-Divide is characterized by a high percentage of flake fragments (65.2 percent), and low percentages of retouched pieces (11.6 percent), and cores (3.2 percent). The flakes, which tend to be small and thin with very little cortex, were produced from locally available coarse-grained materials such as basalt and a quartzitic chert. These characteristics suggest that secondary reduction (including tool production or repair) was the

Figure 3.15 Groundstone artifacts. a-d, hammerstones; e, three-quarter grooved axe (length of e is 12.3 cm).

Figure 3.16 Small artifacts from Townsend-Divide. a-d, sherd disks; e, argillite pendant; f, h, ceramic figurines; g, spindle whorl (length of h is 5.7 cm).

principle task at the site. Secondary reduction is characterized by a high frequency of flake fragments, and a low frequency of complete flakes, retouched pieces and hammerstones, by small, thin flakes with very little cortex, and by a high frequency of lipping and faceted platforms (Rozen 1981: 206).

The projectile points are the only artifacts that can be placed temporally or culturally. The small, serrated obsidian arrow points common to Townsend-Divide are typical of Sinagua assemblages and have been placed in the Pueblo II period. This fits with the dates of the ceramics from the site. There is no indication that there was more than one occupation of the site. These points are much like the long, slender, serrated points found at Snaketown and other Hohokam sites, and influence from the Hohokam or Cohonina is suggested (McGregor 1941). Colton (1946: 290) suggests that the typical Sinagua point is notched. Only one specimen from this assemblage had side notches, but it has been noted that in many cases it is very difficult to distinguish the notch from the serrations of the edges (Smith 1952: 131).

In any case, the individual points show considerable variation in morphology and quality of construction, but have still been considered the same type. It is interesting that 8 of the 10 points are complete, and were found in the vicinity of other complete artifacts. Four of the arrow points, including two blanks, the small triangular point, and a crude serrated point, were found in the vicinity of two pottery vessels, some complete jewelry, and scattered human bone which had been intruded into the fill of Feature 1, and may be part of a disturbed grave assemblage. Two other finely made serrated points were in the fill of Feature 5, along with two miniature vessels, which are commonly found with juvenile burials, and which may also represent disturbed grave goods. The two remaining serrated arrow points and the incomplete dart point were found in the fill of Feature 1, approximately 1 m from the vessels (Feature 6).

The well worn hammerstones are the second artifact type found that are all complete. The shaping of the margins and the heavy spalling indicate repeated use of the implements. Ochre stains, as well as abraded smooth areas, suggest that these implements were used for multiple tasks. Basalt, a dense and heavy material, seems to have been preferred.

The remaining retouched pieces consist of fragmented or unfinished implements and what appear to be exhausted cores. The artifacts are large, crudely made, and bulky, qualities characteristic of implements from Ceramic period sites throughout Arizona (Tagg and Huckell 1984: 92). There is no evidence that extensive tool production was occurring at the site, such as implements with snap fractures, and the number of cores and hammerstones suggests some primary reduction. From the 12 flaked stone artifacts recovered during the testing of the site, including 11 flakes (10 chert and 1 basalt) and 1 obsidian retouched piece, Sullivan (1980: 40) inferred tool making activities, an inference weakly supported by edge damage data.

Ground Stone

A total of 72 pieces of ground stone was recovered from Townsend-Divide. The analysis of these artifacts was handled similarly to the analysis of flaked stone, with a number of metric and nonmetric attributes recorded on each artifact including artifact type, material type, completeness, shape, type of wear, and dimensions.

Methods

Nine artifact types were recognized in the analysis, including manos, metates, abrading stones, polishing stones, grooved axes, palettes, cylindrical shaped stones, and unidentified ground stone. Definitions of these types are based on previous work by Tagg (1984a).

Manos are defined as the hand held unit in the grinding tool combination (Haury 1976: 281), and are typically divided into manos and handstones on the basis of size and shape (Tagg 1984a: 609). Manos include the two-handed type, which is pecked to shape over the entire surface, and loaf-shaped or rectilinear, with length greater than width for use in trough metates. Handstones fit comfortably in one hand, and are usually naturally round or oval river cobbles with little or no intentional shaping. Occasionally called one-handed manos, they are associated with basin metates and preceramic groups.

Metates are the stationary implement in the grinding tool combination, and three subtypes are recognized. Trough metates are characterized by a rectangular use area and straight walls created by the back-and-forth grinding motion of a two-handed mano. Flat metates are large, thick bouldars with a flat area covering one entire surface of the boulder. Small grinding slabs are flat metates which are small enough to be used by a seated person on their lap (Tagg 1984a: 632). Those metate fragments that were too small to identify as to type were placed in an unidentifiable fragment category.

Abrading stones have been defined as tabular pieces of stone, usually sandstone, with both faces flat or slightly concave, which were used to shape an object by abrasion (Woodbury 1954: 98).

Polishing stones are small, unmodified water-worn pebbles exhibiting one or more artificially worn flat surfaces (Woodbury 1954: 96).

Grooved axes are tools designed and used for chopping and were hafted by means of a wooden handle fitted into the groove (Woodbury 1954: 25).

Palettes are small, flat slabs of stone, worn flat or concave on one surface and associated with pigment crushing.

Small cylindrical stones are small stones ground to a cylindrical shape, for uncertain uses.

Unidentified ground stone covers those pieces too small or fragmentary to place in an artifact category.

The lithic material type was recorded for each artifact, and whether it was complete or fragmentary. Wear patterns were defined as either unifacial or bifacial. Length, width, thickness, and shape were recorded on all complete artifacts.

Results

The 72 pieces of ground stone recovered include 18 manos, 15 metates, 5 abrading stones, 1 each of palettes, polishing stones, grooved axes, and small cylindrical stones, and 30 pieces that could not be categorized (Table 3.8).

Table 3.8

DISTRIBUTION OF GROUND STONE

	N	Fea. 1	Fea. 3	Fea. 5	Trench 2	Trench 7	Surface
Manos							
Manos	10	4	1	5			
Blank	1	1					
Handstones	7	3		3	1		
Metates							
Trough	2	1		1			
Flat	2			1			1
Small Grinding Slab	1	1					
Unidentified	10	5		5			
Abrading Stone	5	2		3			
Palette	1	1					
Polishing Stone	1	1					
Grooved Axe	1					1	
Cylindrical Stone	1			1			
Unknown Ground Stone Fragment	30	14	1	15			
TOTAL	72	33	2	34	1	1	1

Manos represent the most abundant identifiable ground stone type (24.0 percent of the assemblage) including 10 manos, 1 mano blank, and 7 handstones. All of the two-handed manos are very similar, but are fragmentary, so dimensions could not be taken. Vesicular basalt was the preferred material with nine pieces (including the blank); the remaining artifacts are sandstone or quartzite. From the fragments, it is apparent that the manos used by the inhabitants of the site were loaf-shaped with unifacial wear and an unused convex surface. Thickness ranges from 2.2 cm to 5.5 cm; most specimens are thin, indicating heavy wear. The sandstone mano has heavy ochre stains on the grinding surface, and light stains on the convex top surface. An interesting note about this artifact is that the sandstone is black from heat or fire, prior to the ochre staining. Two-handed manos are by far the most common type found on sedentary, ceramic period sites, since they were used with the trough metate.

The mano blank is a vesicular basalt fragment with no wear present. The artifact has been ground to shape, exhibiting almost a round profile. This blank resembles manos in the primary or secondary stage of production, such as vesicular basalt manos found at ground stone quarries in the New River region north of Phoenix. The blanks were roughly shaped at quarries and transported to habitation sites for use (Hoffman and others 1983: 9-11).

Of the seven handstones recovered, four are complete and three are fragmentary. All the artifacts are extremely variable. The complete handstones range in size from 8.0 cm to 13.3 cm long, 8.0 cm to 10.0 cm wide, and 3.8 cm to 5.4 cm thick. Four shapes are represented, including triangular, oval, round, and irregular; three have bifacial wear and five are unifacially worn. Raw material types include limestone (4), quartzite (3), and basalt (1). The basalt specimen, a bifacially worked handstone, has ochre stains on one surface. The variability among the handstones can be attributed to variability in the original cobble shapes, since most have not been intentionally shaped. If shaping is present, it is restricted to the edges to produce a more symmetrical form and a better surface for gripping (Haury 1976: 281-282). Handstones were the common grinding tool of preceramic groups (together with the basin metate), but they continued relatively unchanged throughout the ceramic period (Tagg 1984a: 618).

Fifteen metates are represented in the ground stone sample, including 11 fragments too small or eroded to be identified. All of these fragments are from the grinding surfaces of the implements, and include pieces of basalt (4), sandstone (3), rhyolitic tuff (2), and quartzite (1). Those specimens that could be identified include two vesicular basalt trough metate wall fragments, a sandstone flat metate fragment, a rhyolitic tuff flat metate fragment from the site surface, and a complete quartzite small grinding slab. The small grinding slab is irregular in shape, and measures 21.9 cm long by 13.1 cm wide by 7.1 cm thick, with a slightly concave, unifacial grinding surface. It has been suggested that these "lapstones" were used to prepare materials other than food (such as pigments), or that they were large, crude palettes (Gladwin and others 1937: 105; Doyel 1978: 83). The use of quartzite for these artifacts is not uncommon (Tagg 1984a: 633), and may be because of the preference of hard textured material for this artifact type.

Both trough and flat metates were common on sites of this time period, with the trough metate becoming popular in Basketmaker III times and the flat metate appearing in the Pueblo II period (Woodbury 1954: 58). Small grinding slabs have been considered more typical in Pueblo III and Pueblo IV Anasazi sites (Woodbury 1954: 114).

Five artifacts were identified as abrading stones. Four are fine-grained sandstone, the material commonly used for this type of implement, and one is limestone. Four of the abraders are complete: one is square, one is irregular in shape, one is rectangular, and one is oval. They range in size from 3.4 cm to 6.5 cm long, 1.9 cm to 6.0 cm wide, and 1.0 cm to 3.1 cm thick. The complete specimens have flat surfaces, while the fragment has a groove worn in one surface. Many uses have been suggested for these implements, and it seems apparent that they were used for any task that needed an abrasive surface. One of the complete artifacts, the oval specimen (3.4 cm by 1.9 cm by 1.0 cm), appears to be almost too small for use, resembling a miniature mano. It may have been a toy rather than a tool.

One artifact was identified as a palette due to a small concavity pecked into one surface. Although the fragment is vesicular basalt, a material which appears to be too porous for tasks such as pigment grinding, the artifact is very similar to the raised border palettes and grinding slabs defined by Woodbury (1954: 112-116, Fig. 23). The concavity is centered in the fragment, suggesting reuse of a piece of another artifact.

One polishing stone was recovered from the fill of Feature 1. The quartzite pebble fragment has one well-defined flat surface, suggesting heavy or long-term use of the implement.

A complete three-quarter grooved basalt axe was recovered from the backhoe backdirt of Trench 7, where two burials (Features 3 and 7) were located. The fact that the specimen is complete and was recovered in the backdirt near the burials, suggests that it may have been a grave offering for either of the burials. The axe has been pecked to shape and rough smoothed. The groove, made for hafting the implement with a "J" shaped handle, has ridges on either side and is located in the upper third of the artifact (Fig. 3.15e). The top of the poll is flat, and the tip of the bit is slightly spalled and flattened from use. The complete axe is 12.3 cm long, 7.4 cm wide, and 5.0 cm thick. The three-quarter grooved axe is typical for the Sinagua in the Rio de Flag and succeeding phases (Colton 1939: 38-44). It has been associated with the Hohokam, and Woodbury (1954: 30) suggests that it was absent in the Flagstaff area until early Pueblo II times, when there is believed to have been an influx of southern traits.

One small cylindrically-shaped artifact of sandstone was recovered from the fill of Feature 5. The artifact has been shaped on all sides and is 3.7 cm long, 2.2 cm wide, and 1.8 cm thick. It has been suggested that objects such as this were finger-sized pestles, as indicated by such artifacts found associated with stone bowls on archaeological sites (Ferg 1984: 680; see also Franklin [1980: 156] and Fulton [1934a: 21, Plate 17a and 18c, 1934b: 20, Plate 14d]). The end of the specimen from Townsend-Divide has been ground, suggesting a back-and-forth crushing motion, which supports the idea of a miniature pestle.

Finally, 30 pieces of ground stone could not be identified due to their fragmentary or eroded state. All of the pieces exhibit what appear to be ground surfaces. Sandstone (29) and quartz (1) are present. The grinding surfaces varied on the pieces, with most flat and unifacial (19). There are also a few examples of flat bifacial surfaces (5), concave unifacial surfaces (3), concave bifacial surfaces (1), and a bifacial specimen with one concave and one flat surface. These pieces probably represent fragments of artifacts such as manos, metates, or abrading stones.

Discussion

The ground stone assemblage is characterized by implement fragments that have been discarded into the fill of the two pit houses (Features 1 and 5). Only the complete grooved axe may have been *in situ*, but disturbance by the backhoe trench makes this inference weak. Readily available raw material, predominately vesicular basalt and sandstone, was utilized for the manufacture of the implements. The occurrence of ground stone on the site indicates that plant foods were processed on the site, as would be expected from a habitation site. The three-quarter grooved axe, as do the serrated projectile points, suggests trade with or influence from the Hohokam or both or commonality of technology.

Small Artifacts

This section includes artifacts of stone, bone, shell, and clay that were made into both utilitarian or nonutilitarian objects (Table 3.9). Some of the artifacts are included in the artifact counts of like material, such as ceramics or bone.

Worked Bone

A total of six pieces of worked animal bone was recovered, including four awls, one gaming piece, and one perforated bone. The four bone awls, three from Feature 1 and one from Feature 5, include two complete specimens and two fragments. Two of the artifacts, one complete and one fragmentary, represent the most common awl type associated with the Sinagua. They are deer or antelope (artiodactyl) metapodials split through the distal end, then ground and smoothed on

Table 3.9

DISTRIBUTION OF SMALL ARTIFACTS

	N	Fea. 1	Fea. 5
Bowl awl	4		
Split type	2	1	1
Splinter type	1	1	
Fragment	1	1	
Bone gaming piece	1		1
Perforated bone	1		1
Worked ceramics	5		
Spindle whorl	1		1
Figurine	1		1
Sherd disk	3	3	
Stone pendant	1		1
Shell	7		
Bracelet	3	3	
Ring/pendant	1		1
Pendant	1	1	
Valve	1		1
Bead	1		1
TOTAL	19	10	9

the split side to make a better grip and to create a sharp tip (Fig. 3.17a, b) (McGregor 1941: 227, Fig. 74b). The tip of the fragmentary awl has been burned, a process which would harden the bone, and it is heavily polished. The complete awl, 11.3 cm long, also has a polished tip, and appears to have been resharpened many times. This style of awl is present throughout Sinagua prehistory.

The second complete awl, a jack rabbit tibia, would fall under McGregor's (1941: 229, Fig. 74f, g) splinter awl type (Fig. 3.17c). This style usually consists of a splinter of bone from the shaft of a

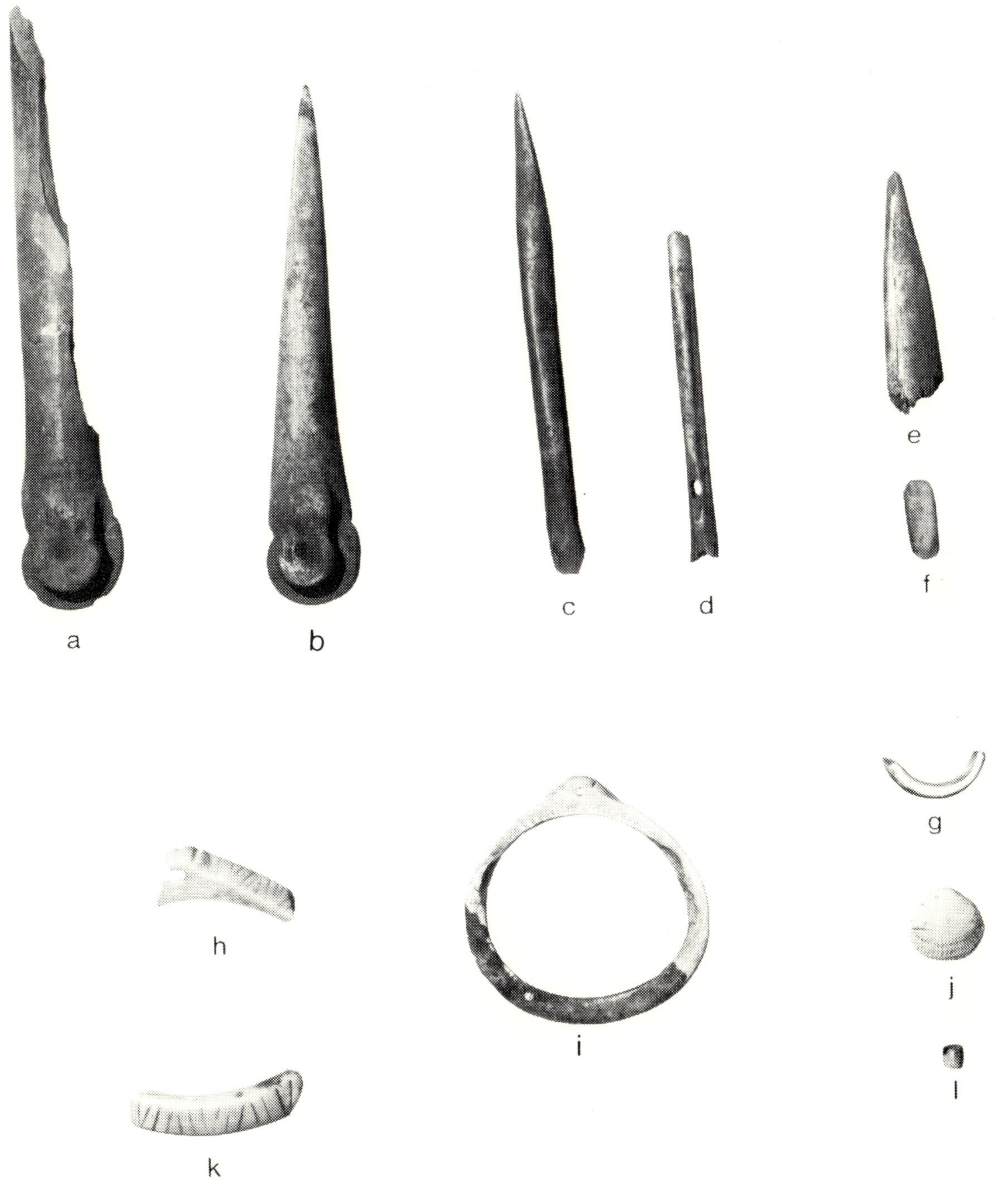

Figure 3.17 Bone and shell artifacts from Townsend-Divide. a, c, e, awls; d, perforated bone, f, gaming piece (?); g, ring/pendant; h, i, k, shell bracelets; j, valve; l, bead (length of a is 13.1 cm).

mammal long bone. Unlike the previous type mentioned, only the proximal end of the bone has been split to create the tip. The remainder of the shaft is intact, with some smoothing or polishing present. The specimen is 10.3 cm long. This style of awl is also present throughout Sinagua prehistory. The remaining awl fragment, which is a fragment of a long bone of a large mammal, is the tip of what appears to have been a large awl (Fig. 3.17e). As with the other specimens, it has been split and smoothed to create a sharp point, but use or weathering has rounded the edges.

One small worked bone has been classified as a gaming piece. The complete artifact, 1.7 cm by 0.7 cm by 0.3 cm, appears to be from a piece of a small mammal long bone that was cut in half and from which the cancellous tissue was removed. The remaining piece was ground to a rectangular shape (Fig. 3.17f). The finished product has one, highly polished flat face and one concave surface (the interior of the bone), giving a shallow U-shaped profile. A similar object was found at one of the Winona and Ridge Ruin Padre phase sites, and was thought to be either a die or perhaps used as a bone inlay in mosaics (McGregor 1941: 233, Fig. 75k). Sets of more elaborate bone gaming pieces with incised surfaces and traces of pitch were found at Sand Dune Cave (NA 7523) in the Navajo Mountain area of Glen Canyon; although these pieces were oval or round and better made, the piece from Townsend-Divide fits well within their size range (Lindsay and others 1968: 58-59). Morris and Burgh (1954, Figs. 95 and 96) also illustrate a wide variety of small bone gaming pieces from Basketmaker II sites.

The remaining bone artifact is a jack rabbit radius with a hole drilled through the shaft near the distal end (Fig. 3.17d). The distal end is smooth where it was broken, and the proximal end was lost during recovery. Various types of bone artifacts from Sinagua sites exhibit drilled perforations, including awls (also called "needles"), whistles, and ornamental objects such as pendants, beads, or earrings (McGregor 1941: 229-232, Figs. 74g and 75c, d, g, l). The nature of the artifact from Townsend-Divide suggests that it was a splinter type awl with a perforation, possibly for suspension (McGregor 1941: 229, Fig. 74g).

Worked Ceramics

Five worked ceramic artifacts were recovered, including a spindle whorl, a figurine, and three sherd disks. The first artifact is a spool-shaped object; it is roughly made with flat, rounded ends (one of which is smaller than the other), a groove around the middle, and a perforation through the center (Fig. 3.16g). It resembles a modern day spool for thread, and is commonly referred to as a spindle whorl on Sinagua sites (Bartlett 1934: 63, Fig. 43f; Colton 1939: 38, Fig. 5f; McGregor 1941: 75-76, Fig. 22d). They are characteristic of the Rio de Flag phase of the Sinagua, although the specimen from Townsend-Divide is more roughly made than shown by Colton (1939: 38, Fig. 5f). Although they have been included as spindle whorls by most investigators, it has also been suggested that they were ear spools, since figurines wearing similar objects have been found. Unfortunately, none has been found with burials to support this theory (Bartlett 1934: 63-64; McGregor 1941: 76). The spool is 1.7 cm long and 1.7 cm wide.

Three perforated sherd disk fragments were recovered from Feature 1. One fragment is a Tusayan Black-on-red sherd that was ground into a round or oval shape (Fig. 3.16a); the second is a Deadman's Fugitive Red sherd that is rectangular in shape--3.6 cm by 2.4 cm by 0.6 cm (Fig. 3.16c); and the third is a Deadman's Gray sherd fragment that was either square or rectangular when complete (Fig. 3.16d). These sherd disks are commonly called spindle whorls, although Colton (1946: 290) suggests that the manner in which the perforation is made, two small conical holes drilled from opposite sides, precludes that function. A Deadman's Black-on-red sherd from Medicine Cave (NA 863) had a knotted rawhide thong through the hole, suggesting use as a button or ornament. Decorated sherds, especially from Kayenta branch pottery types, were preferred for the manufacture of disks (Colton 1946: 291). Round disks, both perforated and unperforated, are the most common form, being seen throughout Sinagua prehistory. Rectangular specimens have also been recovered from Pueblo II sites, however, including some made on Deadman's Fugitive Red sherds (Bartlett 1934: 48, Fig. 34a). A round Sunset Brown perforated sherd disk fragment was also collected from the surface of the site during the testing project (Fig. 3.16b).

A figurine fragment was recovered from the fill of Feature 5. The specimen is the base of a very crude and simple figure: the fragment is a thick column of clay, with two "ears" extending from one end that may represent legs, forming a Y-shaped figure (Fig. 3.16h). Similar figurines have been found in the Prescott area (Gladwin and others 1937, Plate CCXI), and reel-shaped or dog bone-shaped artifacts with matching Y-shaped ends have been recorded from Snaketown (Gladwin and others 1937, Plate CCXI; Haury 1976: 270, Fig. 12.36k), the Hodges Ruin (Kelly 1978: 84, Fig. 58k) and other Hohokam sites in southern Arizona. The fragment is early Angell Brown, indicating that it was made locally.

A second figurine fragment was collected from the surface of the site during the 1980 testing project (Sullivan 1980). It is a style much more commonly found on Sinagua sites. The fragment consists of the head of a human figure, with a flat face and a markedly raised, pinched-up nose. There is no indication of eyes, as the upper portion of the head is missing (Fig. 3.16f). McGregor (1941: 79-81, Fig. 23) describes two types of Sinagua figurines, those with coffee bean eyes and those without, and suggests influence from Prescott or the Hohokam, or both. This type of figurine is further illustrated by Gladwin and others (1937: 233-243, Plates CXCVII and CCVII). The type of figurine recovered from Townsend-Divide is most similar to those from the Santa Cruz phase, and Pueblo II and III times in the Prescott area (McGregor 1941: 80).

Worked Stone

One red argillite pendant was recovered from the fill of Feature 5. This trapezoidal artifact (2.0 cm by 1.5 cm by 0.2 cm) has been ground to shape on both sides and all edges, and has a hole drilled in the small end (Fig. 3.16e). Red argillite pendants such as this are not uncommon in northern Arizona, and although a variety of other lithic materials were used for making ornaments, red argillite seems to have been the most commonly used (McGregor 1941: 195-196). Almost identical specimens were recovered from NA 682 in Wupatki and the Awatovi sites in northeastern Arizona (Smith 1952: 133, Fig. 49; Woodbury 1954: 143, Fig. 29). Various sources of argillite are known to have been exploited prehistorically. A source near Del Rio, north of Prescott, is thought to have been the source of much of the material used in the Flagstaff area. This material can be identified by its distinctive white flecks (Bartlett 1939: 75-79; McGregor 1941: 195); the lack of these flecks in the specimen from Townsend-Divide suggests it is from another source, perhaps the outcrops near Perkinsville in the Verde Valley (Fish 1974: 17), or the source near Jakes Corner in the upper Tonto Basin (Haas 1971; Ferg 1984: 684).

Worked Shell

Seven shell artifacts were recovered from Townsend-Divide including three *Glycymeris* bracelets, a *Glycymeris* ring or pendant fragment, a *Haliotis* washer-shaped geomorphic pendant, a *Glycymeris* valve, and an *Olivella* cylindrical bead (Fig. 3.17g-l). These artifacts are discussed in greater detail in Appendix C.

Chapter 4

INTERPRETATIONS

Subsistence

Environmental and archaeological evidence in the Flagstaff area indicates that the region was only marginal for agricultural practices, but was satisfactory for substantial hunting and gathering activities (Hohman 1982: 71). In the ponderosa pine zone, extending from about 6900 feet to 7300 feet, the major constraint on agriculture was the comparatively short and highly variable growing season (Sullivan 1984: 85). The mean growing season is currently about 116 consecutive frost-free days, which is somewhat above the minimal 110 days needed for profitable maize cultivation. But the variation in the range of frost-free days, from 86 to 151 over the period 1899 to 1934, suggests that significant crop loss due to early or late frosts was always a major risk. The mean annual precipitation of Flagstaff is 19 inches, ranging from about 12 to 34 inches between 1899 and 1955, with an average of 8.1 inches of warm-season precipitation. Successful maize cultivation requires 8.0 inches of warm-season precipitation. This can be considered less of a constraining factor for prehistoric farming because of the relative ease of modifying moisture availability by means of irrigation, check dams, and careful selection of farm sites having favorable soils (DeBoer 1980: 4). During the Preeruptive period, villages tended to be scattered along the margins of the parks, where two farming strategies could have been employed within the parks; dry farming in the center, and floodwater farming along the edges where they are entered by numerous washes from the San Francisco Peaks or surrounding lava flows. Away from the parks, check dams and irrigation ditches were used (Pilles 1979: 463). This location of sites on the fringes of the upper pine zone and lower park areas reflected utilization of a wide range of resources in both environmental zones.

After the ash fall from the eruptions of Sunset Crater, the conditions for agricultural practices improved in some localities. The ash mulch, along with increased summer rainfall and warmer temperatures occuring after A.D. 1100, allowed for a longer growing season, and seems to have provided an environment more suitable to intensive agricultural subsistence strategies (Hohman 1982: 71). This change in conditions allowed the Sinagua to move from the fringes of the ponderosa forests to new locations at lower elevations in pinyon-juniper country (Pilles 1978: 129). Use of the pine zone continued though, even with the decrease of agricultural productivity. Burn-plot agriculture, which consists of intentional burning of plots of organic material to create a fertile field, was utilized (Sullivan 1984: 97-99). This would indicate that Sinagua groups near Mount Elden may have been little effected by the eruptions of Sunset Crater, with subsistence patterns remaining much the same after as they were before the eruption.

The analysis of animal bone and flotation samples recovered from Townsend-Divide (Appendixes B and D) provides evidence of the subsistence of the inhabitants of the site. Recovery of animal bones, agricultural plant remains, and wild plant resources indicates that both agriculture and hunting-gathering were employed by the inhabitants of the site. Agriculture is represented by two cultigens, corn and beans, which were recovered from the fill of both pit houses and one burial. In addition, there is evidence of one possible cotton seed. Although the evidence is equivocal, it may be postulated that cotton seeds were also utilized as foodstuffs (Appendix D). The placement of the site on the edge of Doney Park made the arable Navajo loam readily available for the construction of agricultural fields (Fig. 2.1), and it seems likely that it was utilized for that purpose.

Hunting and gathering are represented by the animal bone and by amaranth and chenopodium seeds (Appendix D), all of which suggests reliance on locally available animals and plants. Small mammals such as rabbits and rodents appear to have been preferred. These creatures would not only be more abundant, but would also be easier prey than the larger mammals, such as antelope or bison. Rabbit drives using nets, which are common to hunter-gatherer groups, would collect large numbers of animals with little effort, and dead-fall traps could be used. This reliance on small game is not uncommon; the same pattern is seen at Winona and Ridge Ruin (McGregor 1941: 256-257).

A small number of bird bones was recovered, and McGregor (1941: 258), working with a much larger collection, suggested that many of the birds may have been collected for their plumage rather than for food. The recovery of fish and mud turtle bones suggests a permanent or intermittent stream or water source in the vicinity, and the recovery of fish and water fowl bones from Winona and Ridge Ruin prompted McGregor (1941: 259-260) to suggest the presence of shallow lakes in the immediate region.

Unfortunately, the information recovered from Townsend-Divide adds little to the knowledge of Sinagua subsistence patterns. The small sample analyzed only indicates that both agriculture and hunting-gathering were present, but sheds no light on the relative importance of either. The location of the site on the edge of the arable Navajo loam and the pine forest puts two environmental zones within easy access of the inhabitants. This strategic placement of the camp to exploit many environmental zones, as well as to give access to permanent water (such as a spring), is a trait well known for hunter-gatherer groups in the western United States (for instance, see Tagg [1984b: 146]). It seems apparent that this strategy was also used by sedentary groups, as indicated by Townsend-Divide.

Chronology

The chronology of Townsend-Divide is derived from the complementary data sets of indigenous ceramics, intrusive cross-dated ceramics, the eruption of Sunset Crater or one of its associated cones, and archaeomagnetic dates from the hearths within both pit houses (Features 1 and 5). Angell Brown dominated the entire ceramic assemblage, accounting for 91.9 percent, and is comprised of early Angell Brown and late Angell Brown. Early Angell Brown, here defined as typologically and technologically more like Rio de Flag Brown, accounted for 28.5 percent of the ceramic assemblage. Late Angell Brown, typologically and technologically more similar to Winona Brown, accounted for 63.4 percent. Colton (1958a) indicates a range of A.D. 1000 to 1150, whereas Breternitz (1966) suggests a range of A.D. 1075 to 1150. Though by no means abundant, intrusive decorated pottery types also fall within this time range. Specifically, the Tusayan White Wares, Little Colorado White Wares, and Tsegi Orange Wares, also support the A.D. 1000 to 1130 or 1150 date range (see Chapter 3, The Ceramic Assemblage).

The presence of volcanic cinders within the fill of both pit houses indicates that they were occupied and abandoned before A.D. 1064 to 1066, that period of volcanic eruptions of Sunset Crater. The cooccurrence of intrusive burials in the fill of these pit houses indicates inferentially, a continued occupation of Townsend-Divide after the initial eruption.

Paleomagnetic samples from both hearths in Feature 1, a pit house, yielded 95 percent confidence interval date ranges of A.D. 970 to 1090 (first option) and A.D. 1060 to 1340 (second option) for Feature 1.1, the upper hearth in Feature 1 and A.D. 1000 to 1090 (single option) for Feature 1.2, the lower hearth in Feature 1. Feature 5.1, the hearth associated with the upper floor of Feature 5, the other pit house, yielded a 95 percent confidence interval date range of A.D. 1000 to 1090 and A.D. 1060 to 1270. The 63 percent confidence level and best fit intervals for these hearths are provided in Appendix E. Although the paleomagnetic date ranges do not provide as tight as chronological control as tree-ring samples might have, they do indicate that inferences regarding the occupation span as determined by the ceramic associations are supported.

External Relationships

The occurrence of a number of nonlocal ceramic types within the Tusayan White Wares, Little Colorado White Wares, Cibola White Wares, and Tsegi Orange Wares as well as two types of Hohokam pottery, Wingfield Plain and Sacaton Red-on-buff, indicates external contacts .

with cultural groups north, northeast, east, and south of the traditionally defined Sinagua. With respect to the overall ceramic assemblage, there are 380 sherds (5.4 percent) that represent nonlocally produced types. It is not clear from this small sample, however, what were the mechanisms and the magnitude of these contacts. It is assumed that trade or some form of exchange occurred, but whether this inferred contact resulted from formalized trade networks or from simple reciprocal exchange cannot be addressed with the Townsend-Divide data. The presence of these ceramic types does not necessarily reflect an influx of migrant peoples into the the Flagstaff region as has been argued by Colton (1946).

The presence of Sacaton Red-on-buff and Wingfield Plain, as well as the projectile point styles, figurines, and architectural attributes of Feature 1, supports the inference of Hohokam influence but not necessarily a Hohokam intrusion. Likewise, it is well known that the white wares and orange wares noted above are widely distributed as trade goods throughout the prehistory of the northern Southwest. Fish and others (1980) have pointed out that much material other than simple trade goods probably was exchanged between the Sinagua and other groups, and that this exchange was highly variable in its magnitude. The data from Townsend-Divide shed no additional explanatory light on the problem of Sinagua external relationships. Nonetheless, the diversity of intrusive traits at Townsend-Divide suggests that research conducted in and around the Flagstaff region may need to consider the role of the Sinagua in a larger trade and exchange network in which not ony goods, but ideologies and other nonmaterial items were the foci of external contacts.

Chapter 5

SUMMARY AND CONCLUSIONS

The investigations at Townsend-Divide revealed evidence of a portion of a Sinagua village occupied between A.D. 1000 and 1100, during the late Rio de Flag and early Angell-Winona phases. The chronological placement of Townsend-Divide (Research Question 1, Chapter 1) was derived from three data sets: indigenous ceramics, cross-dated ceramics, and the archaeomagnetic samples, which support the above date range. It is also suggested that the occupation transcended the A.D. 1064 eruption of Sunset Crater or one of its associated cones. Both pit houses (Features 1 and 5) yielded volcanic cinders within the fill, indicating that they had been abandoned prior to the eruption. That the site was occupied following the eruption of Sunset Crater (Research Question 2 and 3, Chapter 1) is derived from the intrusive burials (Features 2 and 6) in the fill of these pit houses. The intrusive burials suggest a continuity of occupation at the site and inferentially indicate the establishment of new pit houses after the existing two were abandoned. Data to verify Colton's (1936) inferences regarding influx of population are simply not present. Likewise, data are primarily inferential regarding the occupational history of Townsend-Divide, in that it is presumed that new pit houses were built to replace abandoned structures. From this, we tenatively infer that there was no population influx at Townsend-Divide following the eruption of Sunset Crater.

The location of the site on the edge of Doney Park, with arable Navajo loam and pine forests descending off Mount Elden, provided the inhabitants access to at least two environmental zones for exploitation. Agriculture and hunting and gathering are evidenced by the remains of cultigens such as corn and beans, wild plants such as amaranth and chenopodium, and the bones of various animals. The animals and wild plants were probably supplements to agriculture, which would have been affected by the highly variable growing season. Small mammals such as rabbits and rodents dominate the sample and were probably collected through drives and with traps, as opposed to big game hunting techniques. All of the species identified were available locally, within a 10 mile radius of Flagstaff. The occurrence of major springs in the vicinity also made the site more attractive, providing dependable water sources. The recovery of fish and mud turtle bones suggests that shallow lakes, or permanent or semipermanent streams in the region, also were exploited by the inhabitants of Townsend-Divide.

The two pit houses and the burials indicate a rather sedentary village, as opposed to the seasonal field houses common to the region, which were used specifically for managing agricultural fields (see, for instance, Pilles [1978]). It seems likely that the excavated portion of Townsend-Divide belongs to a larger village, although the limited excavations make this a hard conjecture to substantiate (Research Question 3, Chapter 1).

Abundant artifacts were recovered from Townsend-Divide, including ceramics, flaked and ground stone, bone, and shell. One aspect of the ceramic analysis was geared toward dividing Angell Brown into early and later categories as a means for gaining better temporal control. This division was based on previous reasearch conducted by the Coconino National Forest, which has indicated that early Angell Brown is more like Rio de Flag Brown, while late Angell Brown is more like Winona Brown. Unfortunately, the badly mixed stratigraphy made this effort impossible. The decorated ceramics proved interesting though, exhibiting mixtures of technological and stylistic attributes of traditionally defined Southwestern pottery types within Little Colorado, Tusayan, and Cibola white wares. These ceramics also indicated that pottery was coming into the area from the north, northeast, and east. The recovery of Wingfield Plain and a Sacaton Red-on-buff sherd indicates possible trade contacts with Hohokam to the south.

The analysis of flaked and ground stone revealed an assemblage of artifacts made of locally available materials and resembling a sedentary tool assemblage. Manos and metates indicate plant processing, and projectile points suggest hunting activities. The points, although similar in form to Hohokam and Cohonina styles, were all made of obsidian and probably represent locally made examples. Contact and trade is further indicated by these artifact types (Research Question 4, Chapter 1). Serrated projectile points, as mentioned above, are common to the Hohokam, and seem to represent the dominant style at Townsend-Divide. A three-quarter grooved axe, also associated with the Hohokam, was recovered near the burials. Both figurines recovered, consisting of a Y-shaped fragment and a face fragment, are very similar to those from the Prescott area and the Hohokam core areas. Finally, all shell forms are common to the Hohokam, and the absence of manufacturing debris suggests that these artifacts came to the site as finished products.

The features at Townsend-Divide also support the inferences of external relationships with other cultural groups (Research Question 4, Chapter 1). Feature 1, a pit house with a peripheral posthole pattern, is reminiscent of Hohokam houses. Semiflexed burials, such as Burial 2 in Feature 3, are thought to have been influenced by the Kayenta Anasazi. In general, the occurrence of Hohokam-like ceramics, figurines, and other typical southern traits, are synonomous with the Hohokam in the northland. It seems apparent that the Sinagua received trade goods and considerable influence from the Hohokam to the south, and from other groups to the north, northeast, and southeast, but the nature of this contact cannot be further defined, either from this small assemblage or from the few features investigated.

Finally, it must be noted that because only a portion of Townsend-Divide was available for investigations, our conclusions regarding the site are limited (Research Question 5, Chapter 1). For example, Sullivan (1980) indicated that the site extended east under existing Highway 89 and probably south into the Coconino National Forest. While it is presumed that additional data from these areas would have increased our sample, the nature of any additional features remains unknown, as does their spatial and temporal variation. Nonetheless, Townsend-Divide provided useful and informative data regarding the Preeruptive-Posteruptive occupations, external contacts, and subsistence, all of which has been little investigated to date.

Appendix A

OSTEOLOGICAL ANALYSIS OF THE TOWNSEND-DIVIDE HUMAN SKELETAL REMAINS

Marilyn B. Saul

Cultural Resource Management Division
Arizona State Museum
University of Arizona

The remains of six individuals from burial contexts were evaluated for age, gender, stature, cranial discontinuous traits and pathologies. In addition, scattered osseous remains from nonburial contexts were recovered and are listed in Table A.1.

Methodology

All osseous remains were cleaned and, with the exception of ribs and incinerated remains, preserved in polyvinylacetate. Reconstruction was attempted with limited success.

Age assessment was based on dental eruption (Schour and Massler 1941) and dental attrition (Brothwell 1965). Gender was assigned on the basis of skeletal attributes outlined by Bass (1971). Metric data was taken only on intact long bones using formulas derived by Genoves (1967). Cranial discontinuous trait assessment followed the format established by Birkby (1973); Dr. Birkby was also consulted on pathologic evaluation.

All data were recorded on standard osteology inventory forms and cranial discontinuous trait forms supplied by the Human Identification Laboratory at the University of Arizona and are filed at that location. The remains are housed at the Arizona State Museum, University of Arizona.

Results

Burial 1 (Feature 3, Individual A): inhumation of a female aged 17 to 25 years; stature estimated at 150.248 cm to 158.025 cm on the

Table A.1

SCATTERED, NON-BURIAL CONTEXT HUMAN REMAINS

Feature	Bag #	Provenience	Depth	
1	75	N86.7-88.25/E98.2-100	1.8-2.55	left clavicle of an individual of at least 15 years of age
1	88	N86.7-88.25/E98.2-100	2.55-2.90	femur (?) fragment, incinerated hard white
1	185	N89-90/E102-102.8	2.55-2.95	unsided femoral diaphysis fragment, incinerated black/grey; did not articulate with fragment from bag 88.
1	301	N92-93/E102-104	1.55-2.50	femur distal fragment of an individual at least 15 years of age
3	176	N82/E94 SE1/4 overburden	S_1L_1	3 rib fragments; 1 carpel (left capitate) these could belong to either burial 1 or burial 2)
3	168	backdirt of Trench 7	--	1 femur diaphysis fragment; this does not belong to either burial 1 or burial 2, but may belong to burial 3.
5	259	N98/E100	2.35-2.60	2 rib fragments
6	130	N89.2-90/E100.25-101	2.48-2.58	unidentified diaphyseal fragment; black/grey incineration; adult; possibly a humerus

basis of the left femur and tibia; no notable pathologies with the exception of dental pathologies, which included periodontal disease and occlusal and medial interproximal neck carie on the right M2. The occipital was deformed in a manner suggesting cradle-boarding: cranial discontinuous trait assessment is on file.

Burial 2 (Feature 3, Individual B): inhumation of an adult female. Specific age could not be determined due to absence of diagnostic elements; adult age was based on complete epiphyseal fusion. No pathologies were noted. The maxilla and mandible and associated dentition were absent abrogating assessment of dental pathologies. No metric data was obtainable. Cranial discontinuous trait assessment is on file.

Burial 3 (Feature 7): inhumation of a female aged 25 to 35 years. Only dental pathologies were noted, and consisted of periodontal disease, antemortem loss of mandibular first and second molars with subsequent bone absorption, enamel hypoplasia of the mandibular canines, and an occlusal carie on the left M3. The maxilla and associated dentition were not available for evaluation. Metric data was unobtainable. Cranial discontinuous trait assessment is on file.

Burial 4 (Feature 6): inhumation of a child aged 18 months. No pathologies were noted. Metric data was unobtainable. Discontinuous traits were not evaluated due to the age of the individual.

Burial 5 (Feature 2): inhumation of a child aged 6 to 18 months. No pathologies were noted. Metric data was unobtainable. Discontinuous traits were not evaluated due to the age of the individual.

Burial 6 (Feature 4): inhumation of a subadult aged 15 years. Perhaps the most interesting of the burials, it was also the least represented. The very incomplete cranium showed evidence of extensive boney remodeling of the right parietal along the sagittal suture in response to a pathology of unknown etiology. The possibilities include recovery from a trauma that pierced that area of the cranium, or trephination, as suggested by Dr. Walter Birkby of the Human Identification Laboratory. In addition, there was marked diploic thickening with concomitant tabular reduction along the coronal suture on a very small fragment of either the frontal or left parietal. This may be a response to an anaemic disorder (though not Paget's desease), also suggested by Dr. Birkby. The specific etiology is unknown. Absense of the mandible and maxilla abrogated assessment of dental pathologies. No other pathologies were noted. Metric and discontinuous trait assessments were unobtainable.

Nonburial Osseous Remains

The scattered, noncontext human remains are presented in Table A.1 in order of associated nonburial features. They represent a number of individuals.

Appendix B

ANALYSIS OF TOWNSEND-DIVIDE FAUNAL REMAINS

L. Keiko Yoshikawa

Zooarchaeology Laboratory
Arizona State Museum
University of Arizona

An assemblage of 272 bone fragments was analyzed from Townsend-Divide. From the site as a whole, a total of 34 bones (12.5 percent) had been exposed to some degree of heat. A large percentage of the bone, 162 fragments (59.6 percent), could be assigned positive taxonomic identification: one infraclass, two orders, three families, six genera, and seven species could be recognized. Only 13 of the 162 fragments (8.0 percent) showed evidence of having been heated.

Of the distinguishable taxa, it appeared that members of the family Leporidae, in this case the black-tailed jack rabbit and cottontail rabbits, dominated the collection with 95 bone fragments (58.6 percent). Only 10 of the 95 fragments (10.5 percent) exhibited some evidence of being heated.

The remaining 110 bone fragments, 40.4 percent of the total collection, were classified on the basis of potential size of the individual, due to the lack of sufficient diagnostic characteristics. Of these bones, 20 fragments (18.2 percent) had been exposed to some degree of heat.

In terms of modifications or alterations to the bones, six bones exhibited some indication of having been worked or culturally altered.

Methodology

The analysis of the faunal material was accomplished by utilizing the comparative faunal collection of the National Park Service, located in the Arizona State Museum, and the personal collection of Dr. Stanley J. Olsen, University of Arizona. Dr. Olsen identified the fish and reptilian elements, and the identification of the bird elements was completed with the aid of Christine R. Szuter.

The variables recorded for those bones for which a positive taxonomic identification could be assessed included provenience, taxonomic identification, element, portion and percentage of the element, the presence and type of burning, epiphyseal fusion, condition of the fragment, and any other significant modifications.

If the fragment lacked sufficient diagnostic characteristics to warrant a positive taxonomic identification below the level of class, then categories based on size of the animal (small, medium, or large) were employed. At times, it was difficult to discern the actual size range of the animal, and so combinations of these categories were utilized. Also, the category "indeterminate-size" was established for those bones that were so fragmentary that any assignment to any one of the previous categories would have been conjectural. The variables noted for these fragments included provenience, probable size of the individual, possible class of bone (long, flat, irregular, and so forth), presence and type of burning, and any other significant modifications.

At times, substantiation of burning may not be as palpable as one may envision. Bones which have been lightly burned will become light brown in color, which is analogous to the color of some soil stains. However, when osseous material is burned, it will predominantly exhibit a dark brown or black color. When it is exposed to extreme heat and calcined, the bone will become a whitish-blue or gray color, possessing a somewhat chalky texture.

In addition to burning, the degree of ephiphyseal fusion was noted. It was recorded whether or not the epiphyseal caps had completely fused, or if a line of fusion was still apparent. This was noted primarily for the purpose of establishing some selection based on age, since studies of the aging of wild animals by epiphyseal fusion are scarce.

The condition of the bone of the taxonomically identifiable material was rated on a scale from 0 to 2. A rating of 0 indicated that the bone was in a good general condition. Faunal material in good condition exhibited an intact cortical surface and demonstrated no evidence of flaking or cracking. A bone would be considered slightly weathered, a rating of 1, if the flaking and cracking on the cortical surface was not extensive. If the cortical surface was badly weathered and exhibited extensive flaking and cracking, the bone was given a rating of 2, indicating a poor general condition.

The last variable to be noted was any other significant alterations to the bone. This category included such factors as rodent gnawing, pathologies, butcher or cut marks, fresh cuts, and signs of cultural modification.

At Townsend-Divide, none of the bones exhibited any evidence of butchering. However, six fragments did evince indications of cultural modification. There were several different variables which were utilized in enumerating the worked bone and bone artifacts. The variables encompassed several different categories. In general, it was noted whehter the bone was burned, was only smoothed, or was an artifact. In this instance, there were two types of artifacts recorded: awl or hairpins, and a possible gaming piece. If the artifact was an awl or hairpin, the manufacturing technique utilized to shape the bone was noted. Two techniques had been employed: the groove-and-snap technique, and the splinter method. In the groove-and-snap technique, the bone is grooved along its length in two places and then snapped off. In the splinter method, a splinter of bone is fashioned into an awl or hairpin by abrasion.

If striations were visible on the fragment, several variables were then recorded, including overall shape (long, short, shallow, or deep), frequency (the number of marks on the bone), and orientation of the marks relative to one another and to the long axis of the bone if identification of the element was possible.

The minimum number of elements (MNE) was calculated, as opposed to the minimum number of individuals (MNI). Even though they are basically the same concept and computed in the same manner, the MNE considers the possibility that perhaps only a portion of the animal, not the complete carcass, was brought back to the site. The MNE was calculated by counting the number of times a certain portion of an element of one side of the body was registered.

The taxonomic fauna identified at Townsend-Divide is presented in Table B.1.

Description of Taxa

Fish (Pisces)

The members in the infraclass Teleostei, the bony fishes, inhabit a great diversity of econiches throughout the world. It is one of the most varied groups in the animal kingdom, encompassing a large number of genera and species. A total of five fragments was identified as Teleostei gen. et sp. indet. Due to the fragmentary and incomplete nature of the bones, a lower level of taxonomic identification could not be assessed. One of the bones from Feature 6 had been exposed to some degree of heat (Table B.2). The minimum number of elements (MNE) is 1.

Reptiles (Reptilia)

There are two species of the genus *Kinosternon*, the mud turtle, which occur in Arizona; *K. flavescens* (Agassizi), the yellow mud turtle, and *K. sonoriense* (Le Conte), the Sonoran mud turtle (Lowe 1980: 158). The presence of either species is indicative of a permanent or

Table B.1

TAXONOMIC FAUNAL LIST
AZ I:10:30

Pisces	
Class: Osteichthyes	Bony fishes
Teleostei gen. et sp. indet.	Bony fishes, genus and species indeterminate
Reptilia	
Order: Testudines	Turtles
Kinosternon sp.	Mud turtles, species indeterminate
Aves	
Order: Falconiformes	Vultures, hawks, and falcons
Falco columbarius/sparverius	Pigeon/sparrow hawk
Order: Passeriformes	Perching birds
Mimidae gen. et sp. indet.	Mockingbirds and thrashers, genus and species indeterminate
Mammalia	
Order: Lagomorpha	Hares, rabbits, and pikas
Leporidae gen. et sp. indet.	Hares and rabbits, genus and species indeterminate
(?)*Lepus californicus* (Gray)	(?)Black-tailed jack rabbit
Lepus californicus (Gray)	Black-tailed jack rabbit
Sylvilagus sp.	Cottontail rabbits, species indeterminate
Order: Rodentia	Rodents
Rodentia gen. et sp. indet.	Rodents, genus and species indeterminate
Cynomys gunnisoni (Baird)	Gunnison's prarie dog
Spermophilus variegatus	Rock squirrel
Thomomys sp.	Pocket gophers, species indeterminate
Neotoma sp.	Wood rats, species indeterminate
Microtus sp.	Voles, species indeterminate
Order: Carnivora	Carnivores
Canis sp.	Dogs, coyotes, and wolves
(?)*Ursus horribilis* (Ord)	(?)Grizzly bear
Bassariscus astutus (Lichenstein)	Ringtail
Order: Artiodactyla	Even-toed ungulates
Artiodactyla gen. et sp. indet.	Artiodactyls, genus and species indeterminate
Cervidae gen. et sp. indet.	Deer and allies, genus and species indeterminate
Odocoileus hemionus (Rafinesque)	Mule deer

Table B.2

TOTAL NUMBER OF BONES (T), BURNED (B), AND CALCINED (C)
BY FEATURE PER IDENTIFICATION
AZ I:10:30

Identification	Feature 1			Feature 3			Feature 5			Feature 6			Total		
	T	B	C	T	B	C	T	B	C	T	B	C	T	B	C
Teleostei gen. et sp. indet.	2	–	–	0	–	–	1	–	–	2	1* 50.0**	–	5	1 20.0	–
Kinosternon sp.	4	–	–	0	–	–	0	–	–	0	–	–	4	–	–
Falco columbarius/ sparverius	1	–	–	0	–	–	0	–	–	1	–	–	2	–	–
Mimidae gen. et sp. indet.	1	–	–	0	–	–	0	–	–	0	–	–	1	–	–
Leporidae gen. et sp. indet.	0	–	–	0	–	–	1	–	–	0	–	–	1	–	–
(?)*Lepus californicus*	1	–	–	0	–	–	0	–	–	0	–	–	1	–	–
Lepus californicus	43	5 11.6	–	0	–	–	21	2 9.5	1 4.8	7	2 28.6	–	71	9 12.7	1 1.4
Sylvilagus sp.	14	–	–	0	–	–	6	–	–	2	–	–	22	–	–
Rodentia gen. et sp. indet.	0	–	–	0	–	–	1	–	–	0	–	–	1	–	–
Cynomys gunnisoni	0	–	–	0	–	–	1	–	–	0	–	–	1	–	–
Spermophilus variegatus	1	–	–	0	–	–	1	–	–	0	–	–	2	–	–
Thomomys sp.	14	–	–	0	–	–	6	–	–	0	–	–	20	–	–
Neotoma sp.	1	1 100.0	–	0	–	–	2	–	–	0	–	–	3	1 33.3	–
Microtus sp.	1	–	–	0	–	–	0	–	–	0	–	–	1	–	–
Canis sp.	0	–	–	0	–	–	1	–	–	0	–	–	1	–	–
(?)*Ursus horribilis*	1	–	–	0	–	–	0	–	–	0	–	–	1	–	–
Bassariscus astutus	0	–	–	0	–	–	1	–	–	0	–	–	1	–	–
Artiodactyla gen. et sp. indet.	12	1 8.3	–	0	–	–	1	–	–	0	–	–	13	1 7.7	–
Cervidae gen. et sp. indet.	4	–	–	0	–	–	1	–	–	2	–	–	7	–	–
Odocoileus hemionus	3	1 33.3	–	1	–	–	0	–	–	0	–	–	4	1 25.0	–
Small-sized mammal	6	–	1 16.7	0	–	–	4	–	–	1	–	–	11	–	1 9.1
Medium or small-sized mammal	19	3 15.8	–	1	1 100.0	–	10	2 20.0	–	3	–	–	33	6 18.2	–
Medium-sized mammal	6	–	1 16.7	0	–	–	5	1 20.0	–	3	–	–	14	1 7.1	1 7.1
Medium or large-sized mammal	16	3 18.8	1 6.3	0	–	–	1	–	–	0	–	–	17	3 17.6	1 5.9
Large-sized mammal	9	3 33.3	–	0	–	–	3	–	–	0	–	–	12	3 25.0	–
Indeterminate-sized mammal	15	3 20.0	–	0	–	–	2	–	–	4	1 25.0	–	21	4 19.0	–
Indeterminate class	2	–	–	0	–	–	0	–	–	0	–	–	2	–	–
Total	176	20 11.4	3 1.7	2	1 50.0	–	69	5 7.2	1 1.4	25	4 16.0	–	272	30 11.0	4 1.5

* Indicates total number of elements
** Indicates percentage as compared to total number of elements

intermittent stream or other body of water (Stebbins 1966: 82-83). A total of four carapace fragments was identified as *Kinosternon* sp. Even though *K. sonoriense* is the more common species, a specific determination could not be made due to the fragmentary nature of the evidence and the lack of diagnostic characteristics. None of the fragments exhibited any indications of having been heated or modified. The MNE is 1 because several fragments could originate from one carapace.

Birds (Aves)

Falco columbarius (Linneaus), the pigeon hawk, and *F. sparverius* (Linnaeus), the sparrow hawk, are the two species of small hawk residing in Arizona (Robbins and others 1966: 79). The sparrow hawk is the more common form of the two species (Lowe 1980: 192). Both species have adapted to a wide variety of habitats, ranging from open areas to within cities (American Ornithologists' Union 1983: 125-126). Two innominate fragments were identified as either *F. columbarius* or *F. sparverius*. This designation was posited due to the absence of comparative specimens of *F. columbarius* in the faunal collection utilized, and the close proximity in size of the two species; there is an average 4-inch difference reported (Robbins and others 1966 79). Neither fragment exhibited any idications of having been heated or modified. The MNE is 1.

The family Mimidae encompasses the mockingbirds and thrashers. They inhabit a wide variety of econiches throughout the state of Arizona (Lowe 1980: 220-221). One bone, the proximal portion of the humerus, was recovered from Feature 1. The general morphology of the fragment denoted a taxonomic identification within the family Mimidae. However, due to the similar structural morphology within the family, a lower level of taxonomic assessment could not be ascertained. The fragment did not evince any indication of exposure to heat or cultural modification. The MNE is 1.

Mammals (Mammalia)

If a bone could not be identified, it was placed in a relative size class. The criteria for a small mammal is jack rabbit-sized or smaller. A total of 11 bone fragments was evaluated as being from a small mammal. One of these(9.1 percent) exhibited evidence of having been exposed to some degree of heat (Table B.2). One fragment, possibly a long bone, had been worked into a small, rectangular, troughlike object (Table B.3).

A medium-sized or small mammal was defined as coyote-sized or smaller. A total of 33 bones was assigned to this category. Six fragments (18.2 percent) had been exposed to some degree of heat (Table B.2). None of the fragments had been modified.

Table B.3

ALTERATIONS AND MODIFICATIONS OF THE BONES
AZ 1:10:30

Feature	FN #	Identification	Element	Portion	Burned	Rodent Gnawed	Smoothed	Artifact	Whistle	Awl or Hairpin	Manufacturing Technique	Stria-tions	Overall Shape	Frequency	Orientation Relative to Each Other	Orientation Relative to Bone Long Axis	Other Descriptions
1	43	Large-sized mammal	Long bone	Medial	-	-	-	Yes	-	Yes	Groove and snap	Yes	Short, shallow	Several	Parallel	Angled slightly	Tip of awl or hairpin.
	166	Artiodactyla gen. et sp. indet.	Metapodial	Medial-distal	Yes	-	Yes	Possible	-	Possible	Groove and snap	Yes	Short, shallow	Several	Parallel	Angled slightly	Possible portion of awl or hairpin, or object of that type configuration. Missing end.
													Long, shallow	Several			
	292	Artiodactyla gen. et sp. indet.	Metapodial	Medial-distal	-	-	-	Yes	-	Yes	Groove and snap	Yes	Short, shallow	Several	Parallel	Angled slightly	
													Long, shallow		Parallel	Parallel	
5	25	Lepus californicus	Rt. radius	Medial	-	-	-	Yes	Yes	-	-	-	-	-	-	-	Hole toward the distal portion. Smoothed where broken distally. Fresh cut where broken proximally.
	96	Lepus californicus	Rt. humerus	Proximal	-	Yes	-	-	-	-	-	-	-	-	-	-	
	111	Small-sized mammal	?Long bone	?Medial	-	-	Yes	Possible	-	-	-	Yes	Very short, shallow	Several	Parallel	-	Smoothed and rounded on all edges and corners, rectangular
	112	Lepus californicus	Rt. tibia	Medial	-	-	-	Yes	-	Yes	Splinter	Yes	Very short, shallow	Several	Parallel	Angled slightly	
6	130	Lepus californicus	Rib	Proximal-	-	Yes	-	-	-	-	-	-	-	-	-	-	

A coyote-sized animal would constitute a medium-sized mammal. A total of 14 fragments was placed in this category. Only two of these (14.3 percent) exhibited evidence of having been exposed to heat (Table B.2). None of the fragments possessed indications of having been fashioned in any manner.

A medium-sized or large mammal would range between coyote-sized and deer-sized. A total of 17 fragments was assigned to this category. Only four of these fragments (23.4 percent) had been exposed to some degree of heat (Table B.2). None of the fragments had been altered or modified.

A large mammal was deer-sized or larger. A total of 12 fragments was of large mammals. Only three of these fragments (25.0 percent) had been exposed to some degree of heat (Table B.2). One fragment from Feature 1 (FN 43) had been worked (Table B.3).

Twenty-one fragments were of the class Mammalia, but due to their fragmentary condition they could not be assigned to a size range. Four of these fragments, 19.0 percent, had been exposed to some degree of heat (Table B.2). None of the fragments had been modified.

The family Leporidae includes the genera encompassing the hares, *Lepus*, and the cottontail rabbits, *Sylvilagus*. More will be cited concerning the ranges and behaviors of these species in the following sections. One fragment from Feature 5 was identified as one of the leporids, but a more specific determination could not be posited due to its incomplete nature.

One bone fragment from Feature 1 was tenatively identified as *L. californicus* (Gray), the black-tailed jack rabbit. However, due to the bone's incomplete condition, a more positive identification could not be assigned. There were no indications of the bone being subjected to heat or being modified.

L. californicus (Gray), the black-tailed jack rabbit, occurs throughout the state of Arizona (Lowe 1980: 251), inhabiting bushy areas, open plains, and sparsely vegetated deserts (Burt and Grossenheider 1976: 207). They tend to be nocturnal, although the early morning and twilight hours are preferred. Their diet consists of primarily green vegetation. A total of 71 fragments was identified as *L. californicus*. Only 10 of these fragments (14.1 percent) were burned (Table B.2). There does not appear to be any selection for certain portions of the body (Table B.4), but with smaller animals, the entire carcass could easily have been transported back to the site. Two fragments, one from Feature 5 (FN 95), and one from Feature 6 (FN 130), had been gnawed by rodents. Two other fragments exhibit indications of having been culturally modified (Table B.3). The MNE is 4.

Based on present day range maps, there are possibly three species of *Sylvilagus*, the cottontail rabbit, which may occur in the Flagstaff area (Cockrum 1960: 72, 74). These species include *S. floridanus* (J. A. Allen), the eastern cottontail, *S. nuttallii*

(Bachman), Nuttall's cottontail, and S. audubonii (Baird), the desert cottontail (Lowe 1980: 251-252). S. floridanus inhabits heavily brushed areas and edges of swamps and weed patches. S. nuttallii resides in the mountains, areas of loose rocks and cliffs, and in thickets and sagebrush. S. audubonii can be found in the open plains, foothills, and low valleys (Burt and Grossenheider 1964: 219-221). Even though the present distribution of S. floridanus and S. nuttallii is a few miles out of the Flagstaff area, they should not be completely excluded (Cockrum 1960: 72). It is possible that these forms occur nearer to the area but have not been sighted, or they may have been brought into the area.

The members of this genus also are nocturnal, although there is a predilection for the early morning and twilight hours. They are herbivorous, foraging primarily on green vegetation. A total of 22 fragments was assigned to the genus Sylvilagus. As with L. californicus, there does not appear to be a selection for specific portions of the body; however, we are again dealing with a small mammal (Table B.4) None of the fragments had been exposed to heat or modified. The MNE is 2.

The members of the order Rodentia, the rodents, inhabit a wide variety of ecological niches. They are primarily herbivorous, although at times invertebrates, in addition to the vertabrates, will be foraged. Only one tooth fragment from Feature 5 was assigned to this taxonomic designation. No modifications of any sort were discerned on this fragment.

The present day range of Cynomys gunnisoni (Baird), Gunnison's prarie dog, covers the grasslands of central and northeastern Arizona (Lowe 1980: 252). They tend to inhabit mountain valleys and open or sparsely brushy country in elevations ranging from 5000 to 8500 feet (Burt and Grossenheider 1964: 99). Only one fragment from Feature 5 was recovered. It had not been exposed to heat or modified. The MNE is 1.

Spermophilus variegatus, the rock squirrels, can be found, as the name implies, on rocky slopes (Burt and Grossenheider 1976: 97). They are predominately diurnal and construct their dens beneath boulders, or logs, or in burrows (Walker 1975: 711). They occur throughout the state of Arizona at elevations below 6000 feet (Lowe 1980: 252). At the higher elevations, or when winter is severe, they may become inactive or may even hibernate (Cockrum 1982: 78). Two fragments, one from Feature 1 and the other from Feature 5, were recovered. Neither exhibited any indications of having been exposed to heat or having been modified. The MNE is 1.

There are presently two species of Thomomys, the pocket gophers, that occur in the area. These include T. bottae (Eydoux and Gervais), the valley pocket gopher, and T. talpoides (Richardson), the northern pocket gopher. Even though present day range-maps restrict the range of T. talpoides to the Kaibab Plateau area, they can not be entirely excluded from the possibility of use at Townsend-Divide (see discussion

Table B.4

NUMBER OF EACH LAGOMORPH ELEMENT
AZ I:10:30

Element	Leporidae gen. et sp. indet.	(?)*Lepus californicus*	*Lepus californicus*	*Sylvilagus* sp.
Cranium	1	–	–	1
Mandible	–	–	2	1
Cervical Vertebra	–	–	3	–
Thoracic Vertebra	–	–	1	–
Lumbar Vertebra	–	–	–	1
Sacrum	–	–	–	1
Sternum	–	–	1	–
Scapula	–	–	11	6
Rib	–	–	7	–
Humerus	–	–	8	1
Radius	–	–	1	–
Ulna	–	–	6	–
Metacarpal	–	–	3	–
Innominate	–	–	6	2
Femur	–	1	8	4
Tibia	–	–	6	3
Calcaneus	–	–	1	1
Metatarsal	–	–	2	1
Proximal Phalanx	–	–	1	–
Total	1	1	71	22

above of the possible use of *Sylvilagus*). The members of this genus are burrowers and are rarely seen above ground. They are active year round and are generally found in soils that are easily worked, and even slightly moist, although some can be found in rocky conditions, as in the mountains. Being members of the order Rodentia, they are primarily herbivorous (Burt and Grossenheider 1964: 131). A total of 20 bone fragments was recorded. None of the bones evinced any evidence of having been exposed to some degree of heat and none of the bones had been modified in any manner. The MNE is 4.

There are five species of the genus *Neotoma*, the wood rats, that occur in Arizona (Lowe 1980: 256). These species include *N. albigula* (Hartely), the white-throated wood rat, *N. cinerea* (Ord), the bushy-tailed wood rat, *N. mexicana* (Baird), the Mexican wood rat, *N. lepida* (Thomas), the desert wood rat, and *N. stephensi* (Goldman), Stephen's wood rat (Lowe 1980: 256). These species cover a wide variety of ecological niches ranging from desert floors to rock cliffs and mountains (Burt and Grossenheider 1964: 175-178). This great diversity in habitats can be seen in the elevational distributions, which extend from 120 to 9200 feet (Lowe 1980: 256). A total of three fragments was recovered. One fragment (33.3 percent) had been exposed to some degree of heat (Table B.2). None of the fragments had been modified in any manner. The MNE is 2.

According to present day range-maps, only two species of *Microtus*, the voles, inhabit the area; *M. longicaudus* (Merriam), the long-tailed vole, and *M. mexicanus* (Saussure), the Mexican vole (Cockrum 1960: 207, 209). *M. longicaudus* inhabits mountain meadows, streambanks, and sometimes dry situations. In the winter season, they may be found in brushy areas. *M. mexicanus* can also be found in mountain meadows, but they prefer dry situations (Burt and Grossenheider 1964: 198) Only one fragment was recovered from Feature 1. The fragment had not been subjected to heat or modified in any manner. The MNE is 1.

Three species of *Canis*, the doglike forms, may reside in Arizona at this time: *C. latrans* (Say), the coyote; *C. lupus* (Fritsch), the gray wolf; and *C. familiaris*, the domestic dog (Lowe 1980: 257). *C. latrans* and *C. familiaris* can be found statewide, but *C. lupus* is extremely rare and may even be extinct in the state. One maxillary fragment from Feature 5 was recorded. Due to the similarity in morphological features of the three species, it would be difficult, if not impossible, to posit a more specific determination. The fragment had not been subjected to heat or modified in any manner. The MNE is 1.

The range of the grizzly bear, *Ursus horribilis* (Ord), once extended throughout the mountainous areas of the state, but is now extinct in the area (Lowe 1980: 257). They prefer the twilight hours and are omnivorous (Burt and Grossenheider 1964: 49). One femoral fragment from Feature 1 was tenatively identified as *U. horribilis*. This uncertainty is due to the limited number of specimens in the comparitive faunal collection. The fragment had not been exposed to heat or modified in any manner. The MNE is 1.

The ringtail, Bassariscus astutus (Lichenstein), can be found throughout the state at elevations ranging from 120 to 6500 feet in chaparral, rocky ridges and cliffs near water (Burt and Grossenheider 1964: 57; Lowe 1980: 257). They are primarily nocturnal and carnivorous (Burt and Grosseheider 1964: 57). One mandibular fragment from Feature 5 was recovered. It was not modified, nor had it been subjected to heat. The MNE is 1.

The members of the order Artiodactyla, the even-toed ungulates, include the pigs (wild and domesticated), deer, prong-horned antelope, bison, sheep, and other bovines. They browse on a variety of woody vegetation and will also graze on grasses and forbs. A total of 13 fragments was recovered. Due to the fragmentary condition of the bones and the analogous morphological structures throughout the members of the order Artiodactyla, neither a generic nor a specific taxonomic determination could be positively assigned. Only one of the fragments, 7.7 percent, had been exposed to heat (Table B.2). Two fragments, both from Feature 1 (FN166 and 292), had been worked (Table B.3). The small sample size made it impossible to determine whether there had been selection for specific portions of the body (Table B.5).

Table B.5

NUMBER OF EACH ARTIODACTYL ELEMENT
AZ I:10:30

Element	Artiodactyla gen. et sp. indet.	Cervidae gen. et sp. indet.	Odocoileus hemionus
Humerus	1	–	–
Metacarpal	–	–	1
Innominate	–	–	1
Femur	1	–	–
Patella	–	–	1
Metapodial	3	–	–
Medial Phalanx	–	–	1
Antler/Horn Core	8	–	–
Antler	–	7	–
Total	13	7	4

The family Cervidae includes the even-toed mammals possessing annually shed antlers (Burt and Grossenheider 1964: 227). These include deer and elk in this region. Seven antler fragments were recovered, but due to their incomplete and fragmentary condition, a lower level of taxonomic assignment could not be posited. None of the fragments exhibited evidence of having been heated or modified.

The distribution of the mule deer, Odocoileus hemionus (Rafinesque), is statewide at elevations of 250 to 9000 feet (Lowe 1980: 259). They tend to inhabit broken country, open plains, brush, or woods, but are well suited for rough terrain (Hall and Kelson 1959: 1004). They are predominately browsers, but will graze on grasses and forbs (Cockrum 1982: 16). A total of four fragments was recorded. Only one fragment (25.0 percent) had been exposed to some degree of heat. None of the fragments exhibited any indications of having been modified. The small sample size made it impossible to determine whether there had been selection for specific portions of the body. The MNE is 1.

Discussion

In compiling the data from the analysis of the faunal material from Townsend-Divide, it appears that very little can actually be concluded, due to a number of factors. The predominant reason is the relatively small sample size and the paucity of elements exhibiting cultural modification. For instance, of the 272 fragments analyzed, only 6, comprising only 2.2 percent of the total assemblage, evinced evidence of having been modified, and none of the bones exhibited any indications of having been cut. In any case, a more or less tentative conclusion can be advanced on the basis of some apparent patterns of selection.

In terms of faunal composition of the site, there appears to have been a high degree of dependency on the members of the family Leporidae, the hares and rabbits, especially the black-tailed jack rabbit (L. californicus). From the site as a whole, a total of 71 fragments has been identified as black-tailed jack rabbit, comprising 26.1 percent, or a little over one-quarter, of the total collection. The distribution per feature of the black-tailed jack rabbit also follows this pattern, as illustrated in Table B.6.

Among the large quantity of black-tailed jack rabbit elements, 2 fragments had been worked (Table B.3), and 10 fragments showed definite signs of having been burned (Table B.2).

The next highest aggregation of bones was that of the cottontail rabbits (Sylvilagus sp.). A total of 22 fragments, or 8.1 percent of the total assemblage, was recorded. In this case, however, it is difficult to ascertain any pattern of dependency on this form due to the lack of bones exhibiting any signs of modification or exposure to heat.

Table B.6

DISTRIBUTION OF BLACK-TAILED JACK RABBIT ELEMENTS PER FEATURE

Feature	Number of Fragments	Percentage of Feature Assemblage
1	43	24.4
5	21	30.4
6	7	28.0

The only other group that included worked elements was the order Artiodactyla. However, a lower level of taxonomic determination could not be assigned.

From this evidence, it appears that the black-tailed jack rabbit and the artiodactyls dominated the resource base. This pattern of dominance is similar to that documented several prehistoric as well as modern Indian groups in the region. However, it would be difficult to conclude that these two taxonomic groups were the only ones to be utilized in such a manner. It is possible that other groups were also employed for some purpose but have not been preserved.

It is a bit more difficult to say just how the animals were butchered and prepared. This is mainly due to the absence of butcher marks or cut marks on the bones of any of these animals. However, if there was a high degree of dependency on such small animals as the black-tailed jack rabbit, then the occurrence of processing scars would be limited. Rarely will bones of small mammals exhibit the characteristic cut marks discernable on larger mammals.

With regard to burning, it is interesting that of the 20 taxonomically identified groups, only 5 (25.0 percent) showed evidence of exposure to heat. These five groups include the boney fishes (Teleostei), the black-tailed jack rabbit (*L. californicus*), the wood rats (*Neotoma* sp.), the artiodactyls, and the mule deer (*O. hemionus*). In other words, out of an assemblage of 162 taxonomically identifiable bones, only 14 fragments (8.6 percent) had been heated to some degree.

The minimum number of elements recorded for the site was 23. The black-tailed jack rabbits and the pocket gophers accounted for the greatest MNE value; both had MNE values of 4 (17.4 percent of the total MNE value).

In terms of environmental indicators, the presence of fish and mud turtle elements suggests a permanent source of water nearby. The rest of the fauna appears to have been quite similar to the modern fauna of the region.

Appendix C

SHELL

Arthur W. Vokes

Cultural Resource Management Division
Arizona State Museum
University of Arizona

The Townsend-Divide site produced seven artifacts of shell from the excavations. These include three bracelets (one of which was a complete specimen), a ring or pendant fragment, a washer-shaped geomorphic pendant, a cylindrical bead, and a largely complete *Glycymeris* valve. The dominant genus at the site is *Glycymeris*, as five of the artifacts were manufactured from it. Unfortunately, the species employed could not be determined for any of these specimens, although the size of the specimens used for the bracelets indicates the source of the raw material was the Gulf of California, as the species native to the California coast are too small to have served this function. The univalve *Olivella* is found both in the Gulf and along the Pacific coast. The valve employed may have been a juvenile *O. dama*; however, all the diagnostic features are missing. There are several other less common species of *Olivella* from both oceanic provinces that also could have been employed. The geomorphic pendant was made out of *Haliotis*, a genus that is exclusive to the California province. A section of the nonnacreous cortex was preserved and the coloration suggests the species was *H. rufenscens*.

Each bracelet was decorated in some fashion. Two fragmentary specimens were recovered from the fill of Feature 5, a pit house. Both specimens were decorated through the use of a stepped-chevron design, which alternated around the band. Both pieces probably are from the same bracelet; one is from the side margin of the valve and the other includes parts of both the umbo and the contiguous dorsal margin (Fig. 3.17*h*, *k*). The umbo has been perforated by grinding back the plane of the taxodontic teeth. There is no evidence of any further finishing of the perforation such as might have been pursued if it was to be used for suspension. The third specimen is a complete bracelet recovered from the floor of the same structure (Fig. 3.17*i*). The umbo is the only portion of the bracelet that has been decorated. The motif is a series of three grooves cut into the margins in an alternating sequence. The umbo also has been perforated, in this case by drilling. The maximum external measurement of the bracelet is 53.2 mm. The inner diameter is, at its greatest point, 43.6 mm. The band is 4.0 mm at its widest nondorsal point. It has been argued that bands of this size could not have functioned as bracelets (Pailes 1963: 174; Officer 1978: 116-117). However, specimens this size have been found in association with burials where they were encircling the lower arm (Doyel 1979: 19; Vokes 1983: 507). The presence of the drilled perforation in the umbo gives circumstantial evidence that this specimen may have been suspended. On the basis of the current information this determination can not be made.

A *Glycymeris* ring or pendant was recovered from the fill of Feature 5, the second pit house. It is approximately one-third of the band, including portions of the side and ventral margins, and is 5.5 mm in width (Fig. 3.17*g*). The inclined outer surface of the natural valve has been ground away to produce a vertical face. The inner margin is characterized by a pronounced ridge that projects into the central aperture. It has been argued that this characteristic, often found on these artifacts, suggests their use as pendants rather than as finger rings (Vokes 1983: 514). Burials at the late locus of San Cayetano del Tumacacori were found with this artifact in association with established bead forms *in situ* about the neck (Di Peso 1956: 92).

One bead was recovered from the floor of Feature 5. This specimen is a cylindrical bead manufactured from an *Olivella* valve (Fig. 3.17*l*). The entire spire has been removed by grinding and the body whorl has been truncated a short distance below the anal canal.

A geomorphic pendant, made from *Haliotis*, was recovered from the lower fill of Feature 1. The specimen is a washer form with a single perforation through the band. Unfortunately, no measurements could be obtained, as the specimen was badly damaged after excavation.

The final shell artifact to be discussed is an extremely weathered *Glycymeris* valve that was recovered from the upper fill of Feature 5 (Fig. 3.17*j*). The specimen is from a juvenile mollusk. Valves of this size were often employed by the Hohokam as whole shell beads. The form generally is limited to the Classic period. The umbo and margin are missing and the remaining portions are so weathered that determination as to any human modification is impossible. The location of the valve above the cobble fill of the structure suggests that this piece was not associated with the occupation of the structure, probably having been introduced after its abandonment. Its weathered condition indicates it has been exposed to the elements for a considerable period of time.

The presence of human bone in the fill of both structures raises the possibility of a mortuary context for some of this material. The specimen for which this seems to be most likely is the geomorphic pendant, as it was recovered in close proximity to the human bone (Feature 6) in Feature 1. The remaining specimens were sufficiently distant in either vertical or horizontal measures to indicate there was no intentional association.

The absence of any manufacturing residue or raw material, as well as the nature of the artifacts, suggests that the shell material was acquired as finished products (Fish and others 1980). This is typical of the majority of the reported Sinagua settlements. Within the immediate environs of the San Francisco Peaks, the only excavated sites that appear to have been involved in the manufacture of shell products are those in the Winona Village-Ridge Ruin complex (McGregor 1941: 221), and Wupatki (Stanislawski 1963: 346). The Winona sites are generally thought to have been the focus of the Hohokam influences and are seen as being atypical of the Sinagua pattern. Wupatki, being the largest regional center, naturally would have been a focus of exchange systems operating in the area. The artifactual forms recovered at Townsend-Divide could easily have been assimilated by these larger assemblages. The incised bracelet fragments recovered in Feature 1 are very similar to specimens illustrated by McGregor (1941: Plate 73). Furthermore, the Olivella cylindrical bead form was the most commonly recovered form in the Winona Village and Ridge Ruin assemblage (McGregor 1941: 216). Whether or not the actual source for the current material was the Winona complex can not be determined. However, it does seem evident that the ultimate impetus was from the Hohokam culture. The existence of an extensive exchange network between the Sinagua and the Hohokam heartland has been recognized for some time (Colton 1941: 7; Stanislawski 1963: 349; McGuire and Downum 1982). All the recovered specimens represent forms that were widely distributed throughout the Hohokam area during the same span of time in which Townsend-Divide was occupied.

Appendix D

ARCHAEOBOTANICAL REMAINS FROM TOWNSEND-DIVIDE

Lisa W. Huckell

Cultural Resource Management Division
Arizona State Museum
University of Arizona

Twenty-eight samples from Townsend-Divide were submitted for archaeobotanical analysis. They consisted of 19 flotation samples, 5 plant macrofossils, and 4 pieces of wood charcoal. These samples were obtained from five features, which included two pit houses (Features 1 and 5), two human burials (Features 3 and 7), and a vessel cache found in Feature 1 that was thought to be associated with a burial (Feature 6). The inventory of plant taxa recovered includes such staples as corn and beans, along with various wild species locally available to site inhabitants.

Methods

The flotation samples were processed using the method presented by Bohrer and Adams (1977: 37). Sample sizes ranged from slightly less than 200 ml to 4220 ml. The dried residues were then sorted using a stereo-zoom dissecting microscope with magnification capabilities of 7X to 30X. With the exception of one sample from the floor of Feature 1, 100 percent of each sample was examined. Any carbonized item that appeared to have any potential for identification was removed and set aside for additional study. Modern seeds and plant parts were also segregated in order to provide some idea of feature disturbance and to help suggest the kinds of plants that have grown in the site area in recent times. Identifications were confirmed through comparison with modern plant specimens in the author's collection.

Wood charcoal was examined using two incident-light microscopes made available by the Laboratory of Traditional Technology, Department of Anthropology, University of Arizona. One was an Olympus DHMJ microscope with a magnification range of 50X to 750X, the other a Zeiss SR stereoscope, with magnification capabilities of approximately 3X to 98X. The charcoal samples were either snapped or split with a razor blade to produce fresh cross, radial, and tangential surfaces. The specimens were then identified using wood keys (Panshin and de Zeeuw 1980) and comparative samples in the author's collection. Due to the time-consuming nature of this identification process and the desire to avoid excessive duplication of effort, those samples with multiple pieces were themselves sampled. Criteria for selection were primarily size or structural integrity or both.

Results

Results of the analysis revealed a total of 12 identifiable taxa in the combined samples. They are presented in Table D.1. Table D.2 presents the number of specimens for each taxon by provenience. Four flotation samples, one from Feature 1.1 and three from Feature 1.2, contained no identifiable items; as a result, they are not included in the table.

Flotation and Macrofossils

The materials recovered by means of the flotation process were fairly consistent from sample to sample. The most abundant constituents were rootlets, cinders, fecal pellets, insect exoskeletal fragments (especially those of ants), charcoal, pine needle fragments, sherds, flakes, and a few tiny bones and claws from lizards or small mammals.

The condition of most of the recovered macrofossils ranged from fair to poor. In addition to having undergone the stresses induced by intense heat, the carbonized remains had also been broken into smaller pieces. Almost all of the wood charcoal encountered in the sorting was finely comminuted, precluding the chance of taxonomic identification. Because most of the corn had been reduced to kernel fragments or dissociated glumes and cupules, as well as to smaller fragments, it is probable that some of the unknowns listed in Table D.2 are maize fragments. Paradoxically, in the cases of the cob segments recovered, preservation is excellent, especially for such fragile structures as glumes and cupule hairs. With the exception of the maize cobs, the carbonized macrofossils were generally lacking in such critically important diagnostic features as complete dimensions, seed coats, and surface topography.

Two, or possibly three, cultigens were represented among the plant remains: maize, beans, and possibly cotton. Maize is by far the most abundant plant present, with 327 cob fragments, cupules, glumes, and kernel fragments. The four cob fragments are from the midsection area, and range in completeness from a single row of vertically articulated cupules to a segment with an intact circumference. Data for the cobs are presented in Table D.3. In addition to the raw data, Table D.3 includes a shrinkage compensation factor of 20 percent for cupule width,

Table D.1

INVENTORY OF PLANT TAXA RECOVERED

Gramineae
Zea mays L. corn

Leguminosae
Phaseolus cf. *vulgaris* L. common bean

Malvaceae
cf. *Gossypium hirsutum* var. *punctatum* cotton

Amaranthaceae
Amaranthus spp. amaranth, pigweed

Chenopodiaceae
Chenopodium sp. chenopod, goosefoot

Pinaceae
Pinus spp. ponderosa pine
Pseudotsuga menziesii (Mirb.) Franco. Douglas-Fir

Cupressaceae
Juniperus sp. juniper

Fagaceae
Quercus sp. oak

Portulacaceae
Portulaca sp. purslane

Cleomaceae
Cleome ca *serrulata* Pursh. rocky mountain beeplant

Compositae

as suggested by Cutler (1966: 23), which makes data on these cobs comparable to cob data published by Cutler in numerous sources.

Of the many cob characters identified and studied over the years, two of the most easily obtained and most informative features are row number and cupule width. Row number is simply the number of vertical rows of kernels present on the cob. It generally tends to decrease over time, with higher frequencies of 12-rowed and 14-rowed cobs gradually being replaced by a greater percentage of 8-rowed cobs (Cutler 1966: 11). The cupule is a depression in the cob that usually bears two florets, each of which produces a single kernel. In the

Table D.2

PLANT REMAINS FROM AZ I:10:30 (ASM)

		Carbonized																		Modern							Charcoal							
Provenience	Sample Type	Maize Cobs	Maize Cupules	Maize Glumes	Maize Kernel Fragments	Maize Fragments, No ID	Bean Cotyledons	Cf. Cotton Seed	Amaranth Seeds	Chenopod Seeds	Cheno-Am Seed Fragments	Cf. Pine Nut Kernel Fragment	Grass Florets	Pine Needles	Pine Needle Spur Shoots	Douglas-Fir Leaves	Juniper Leaves	Twigs; Spines	Unknowns	Purslane Seeds	Chenopod Seeds	Cf. Chenopod Seeds	Amaranth Seeds	Cf. Amaranth Seeds	Composite Achenes	Beeweed Seed	Pine	Oak	Juniper	Douglas-Fir	Hardwood	Unknown	% Fragments Analyzed	Total
F1; house floor*	F		8	2	1																				1									12
F1; house floor	F		24	4		4	1	1						4		1			25				3	2										69
F1; S_1L_2	C																										3	4			2	1	(26)	10
F1; S_1L_2	C																										5						(56)	5
F1; ash lens	F		7	2	2	12			4	3				17	4			4	33															88
F1.1; upper hearth fill	F		3	8															3						1									15
F1.2; lower hearth fill	F								2																									2
F1.2; lower hearth fill	F								6								1		5															12
F1; S_1L_2	M	3																																3
Total		3	42	16	3	16	1	1	12	3	-	-	-	21	4	1	1	4	66	-	-	-	3	2	2	-	8	4	-	-	2	1		216
F3; over-burden	M	-	-	-	-	-	1	-	-	-	-	-	-	-	-	-	-	-	-	-	-	-	-	-	-	-	-	-	-	-	-	-		1
F5; S_1L_2	C																												6				(100)	6
F5; $S_{20}L_1$; house floor	F		7		1				2					1					4	1	2			1		1								20
F5; S_2L_1; lower floor	F		4		1	1					3			1					3	5	1				3									22
F5; S_2L_1	C																													5			(16)	5
F5.1; hearth	F		13		4	5			2						1	2			2															29
F5.6; pit	F		1	2	3																													6
Total			25	2	9	6	-	-	4	-	3	-	-	2	1	2	-	-	9	6	3	-	-	1	3	1	-	-	6	5	-	-		88
F6; S_1L_1	M	1																																1
F6; Vessel 1 fill	F		94	43	34	13	1		30			1	4	13	3	46	20	8	105	3		3	9				4	1					(100)	435
F6; Vessel 3 fill	F		2						6							2	4		3				1											18
Total		1	96	43	34	13	1	-	36	-	-	1	4	13	3	48	24	8	108	3	-	3	10	-	-	-	4	1	-	-	-	-		454
F7; Vessel 1 fill	F		6	1															1									2					(100)	10
F7; Vessel 2 fill	F		2													2			3	2	1		4											14
F7; Under burial	F		9											1					2	14	14			14	1		1						(100)	56
Total		-	17	1	-	-	-	-	-	-	-	-	-	1	-	2	-	-	6	16	15	-	4	14	1	-	1	2	-	-	-	-		80
Grand Total		4	180	62	46	35	3	1	52	3	3	1	4	37	8	53	25	12	189	25	18	3	17	17	6	1	13	7	6	5	2	1		839

* Sampled, not sorted

(F = Flotation; C = Charcoal; M = Macrofossil)

absence of kernels on cobs, row number may be ascertained by counting the number of vertical cupule rows and multiplying by two. Like row number frequencies, cupule width also changes through time. Early maize cupules tend to have narrower, trapezoidal to arch-shaped outlines, while those of later corn varieties or races possess cupules that have become broadened and vertically compressed, exhibiting a rectangular shape.

Of the three cobs from Townsend-Divide for which row number can be counted, all appear to be from 12-rowed cobs. However, it should be kept in mind when considering these data that all of the cob fragments were found in the fill of a single pit house, which raises the possibility that some of the pieces could be from the same cob.

The cupule width data suggest that two distinct types of corn are present at the site. As Table D.3 shows, one cupule width is considerably larger than the others (8.25 mm as compared to 4.51 mm to 5.7 mm). Comparison of the corrected width with similar cob data presented by Cutler (1960: 278, Fig. 2) for Waterfall Cave, Chihuahua, Mexico, and for selected Southwestern sites, indicates that this cob may belong to the Pueblo maize race, while the remaining cobs fall closer to the Pima-Papago maize race, with an average width of 6.11 mm. Loose cupules found in the flotation samples tend to support this dichotomy.

Table D.3

CARBONIZED MAIZE COB DATA, INCLUDING ESTIMATED 20 PERCENT SHRINKAGE COMPENSATION FACTOR FOR MAIZE CUPULE WIDTH

	Row Number	Cob Length (mm)	Cob Width (mm)	Average Cupule Width (mm)	Average Cupule Width + 20% (mm)	Average Cupule Height (mm)
Feature 1 S_1L_2	12	21.0	13.0	4.51	5.41	2.08
Feature 1 S_1L_2	-	8.9	5.9	5.1	6.12	1.7
Feature 1 S_1L_2	cf.12	10.0	13.5	8.25	9.90	1.54
Feature 6 S_1L_1	12	27.5	17.0	5.7	6.8	1.6

A noteworthy feature on some of the cupules is the presence of cupule hairs. These delicate hairs of variable length and density are found along the base of the cupule behind the upper glumes, in the pulvinus notches located at the bases of the flared lateral cupule margins (rachis flaps), and occasionally along the cupule roof or rachis flap margin. The hairs are so variable that they offer little diagnostic potential by themselves; they are most useful when considered with a number of diagnostic traits as a means of securing a determination of race.

The glumes or chaff that surround the kernels can also provide some additional information. The upper glumes in the Townsend-Divide maize are thin and fragile, with most of the outer edges broken away. They appear to be smooth in texture, lacking a conspicuous venation pattern. The lower glumes are thick and firm, curving gently upward like a broad, shallow scoop, and ending in a rounded margin. These long, cup-shaped, durable glumes suggest that there is some teosinte introgression among the maize at the site (Galinat and others 1956). Some specimens still bear long delicate hairs along the lateral margins.

Kernels are represented primarily by small fragments of the upper portion of the grains. Feature 6 yielded the only clues to the shape of the kernels, in the form of a base still bearing the intact embryo, and a partial kernel that includes the top and parts of the sides. This last specimen has a maximum width of 8.1 mm and a thickness of 5.8 mm. It suggests a broad, wedge-shaped kernel with a contracting base. The internal starch visible on the broken grains indicates that they are flour corn.

A good summary of the development of maize races and their subsequent spread through the Southwest is presented by Cutler (1960). What the modest assemblage of corn from Townsend-Divide suggests is that two types of maize were being used by the inhabitants of the site. One may be considered part of the Pima-Papago race, a highly variable race containing both flint and flour corns that show morphological diversity. Many of these types were grown, until the last few decades, by Papago farmers. The second race of corn appears to be Pueblo corn, which includes dented and flour forms, and which made its debut in the Southwest around A.D. 1000. By A.D. 1100, its range had greatly increased. It is still being grown in the Upper Rio Grande Valley of New Mexico.

Beans were also present in the plant macrofossil assemblage from Townsend-Divide, in the form of one cotyledon and two small cotyledon fragments (Table D.2). The complete cotyledon is reniform in shape with blunt, rounded ends. It is 10.8 mm in length, 6.8 mm in width, and 2.6 mm in thickness. The seed coat is gone, having taken with it the diagnostic features around the hilum. However, based on the specimen's size and shape, it is in all probability a kidney bean (or common bean), Phaseolus vulgaris (Kaplan 1956: 205). Kidney beans, along with lima beans and teparies, have been found at other Sinagua sites (Jones 1941: 297-298; Stanislawski 1963: 466, 470).

The presence of cotton at Townsend-Divide is based on the tentative identification of a single damaged seed found on the floor of Feature 1. The seed is elliptical in outline, and measures at least 6.3 mm in length and 3.9 mm in width. Part of the seed is missing, making an accurate thickness measurement impossible. Despite surface blistering and pitting, the seed has retained enough features to suggest the possibility that it is cotton.

Cotton was an important commodity to the Sinagua, who developed an elaborate textile industry centered around the weaving of this fiber (Kent 1954; Stanislawski 1963: 453-466). In addition to the valuable fibers, the seeds also saw use among some aboriginal groups as a food item. The Pima and Papago parched the seeds for a popcornlike snack and mixed the ground seed meal with other foods to create a variety of dishes (Castetter and Bell 1942: 198). Although environmental conditions in the Flagstaff area probably precluded the possibility of growing cotton locally, seeds, fibers, and textiles could have been acquired from other Sinagua villages situated at lower elevations.

In addition to the domestic plants present at the site, some wild plant products were also evident. Chief among them is amaranth, of which 52 seeds were found (Table D.2). Virtually all the seeds are incomplete; most are missing the encircling embryo, lost as the starchy endosperm expanded in response to intense heat. A few of the seeds are larger than the rest, suggesting the possibility that two species may be involved. Amaranth seeds have been extensively exploited for food by both prehistoric and historic cultural groups. The tiny seeds are nutritious and tasty, and can be efficiently collected in large quantities with seed-beating equipment. The young plants have also been harvested for use as a green or pot herb.

Three chenopod seeds were found (Table D.2); they have been used in the same manner as the amaranth seeds. The remaining carbonized items in Table D.2 are mainly leaves, conifer needles, twigs, spines, or unknowns. The exceptions are some grass florets and a possible fragment of the kernel of a pinyon pine nut from the same provenience in Feature 6. However, the bean fragment and the large quantity of maize and unknowns from Vessel 1 in Feature 6 (Table D.2) suggests that this vessel may have contained food residues or trash at the time it was left. Pine, juniper, and Douglas fir are important ceremonial plants among the Hopi (Whiting 1966: 62-63), so it may be that the foodstuffs and leaves were left as offerings. It is impossible to interpret, from the evidence at hand, the significance of the variety and quantity of leaf and needle types. There is no way to distinguish items introduced by animals or insects, or by natural forest deposition, from those introduced by human activity.

A few words should be said regarding the "unknown" category. This heading includes any carbonized item bearing one or more surfaces or features that could lead to an identification. A shortage of time precluded a thorough or exhaustive effort to achieve the most specific identification possible. There is little apparent duplication among the bits and pieces; in all liklihood, corn is the largest taxon represented.

The unburned seeds found in the samples (Table D.2) are assumed to be recent in age. Carbonization is generally taken to be the best indicator of those plant products probably used prehistorically (with the exception of agricultural products, which are inextricably tied to humans). Carbonization also greatly increases the preservation potential for plant parts, especially in open sites where unburned plant parts would be expected to deteriorate rapidly. Despite the fact that all of the modern genera recovered from Townsend-Divide are known to have had economic significance from both ethnographic and archaeological evidence, they are also the same foods collected by insects and animals. The presence of large numbers of seeds, such as those under the Feature 7 burial (Table D.2), can help indicate disturbed, bioturbated areas.

Charcoal

Thirty-four pieces of wood charcoal were analyzed (Table D.2). All were completely carbonized, except for the Douglas fir wood from Feature 5. This is a single large branch fragment that still bears patches of brown wood, and is probably of recent origin. Pine, oak, and juniper are all readily available locally and would have provided a choice of structural and fuel woods to aboriginal inhabitants of the site. Unfortunately, there is no way to relate the recovered woods to a specific function within the features, and no good pieces of charcoal were found in postholes or hearths.

Summary

Townsend-Divide yielded evidence for the use of two domestic plants--maize and beans. It is possible that two varieties or races of corn are present in the small sample of cobs and intact cupules. The common bean, although not well represented in the sample, was probably an important dietary staple along with corn. A single seed of what may be cotton suggests that the site residents had contact with neighboring villages where this plant could be grown. Seeds of two wild plants, amaranth and chenopod, may have been gathered as dietary supplements.

Appendix E

ARCHAEOMAGNETIC DATA REPORT

Barbara A. Murphy

Paleomagnetism Laboratory
Department of Geosciences and
Arizona State Museum
University of Arizona

Feature 1.1

Provenience: AZ I:10:30, ASM, Feature 1.1 (upper hearth in Feature 1)
Site Location: T22N R8E Section 33, SW-1/4 NW-1/4 NW-1/4, Zone 12, E449200 N3900900
Magnetic Declination: 10.95 degrees
Latitude: 35.20 degrees
Longitude: 248.37 degrees

Paleomagnetic Results

Alternating field used for demagnetization (EXP): H150 oersteds
Number of samples submitted: 11
Number used for interpretation (N): 11
Mean magnetization (J): 2.79E-03 gauss
Mean paleomagnetic inclination (I): 60.15
Mean paleomagnetic declination (D): 348.22
Radius of 95 percent circle of confidence about mean direction: 3.0
Precision parameter (k): 232.25
Virtual geomagnetic pole latitude (PLAT): 79.05
Virtual geomagnetic pole longitude (PLONG): 194.24
Semimajor axis of 95 percent oval of confidence about pole position (DM): 4.55
Semiminor axis of 95 percent oval of confidence about pole position (DP): 3.44

Interpretations

95 percent confidence level: A.D. 970-1090, A.D. 1060-1340
63 percent confidence level: A.D. 1030-1080, A.D. 1070-1270
Best fit interval: A.D. 1130-1180

Feature 1.2

Provenience: AZ I:10:30, ASM, Feature 1.2 (lower hearth in Feature 1)
Site Location: T22N R8E Section 33, SW-1/4 NW-1/4 NW-1/4, Zone 12, E449200 N3900900
Magnetic Declination: 10.00 degrees
Latitude: 35.20 degrees
Longitude: 248.37 degrees

Paleomagnetic Results

Alternating field used for demagnetization (EXP): H100 oersteds
Number of samples submitted: 10
Number used for interpretation (N): 10
Mean magnetization (J): 4.05E-03 gauss
Mean paleomagnetic inclination (I): 64.12
Mean paleomagnetic declination (D): 349.03
Radius of 95 percent circle of confidence about mean direction: 2.7
Precision parameter (k): 311.84
Virtual geomagnetic pole latitude (PLAT): 76.49
Virtual geomagnetic pole longitude (PLONG): 213.82
Semimajor axis of 95 percent oval of confidence about pole position (DM): 4.37
Semiminor axis of 95 percent oval of confidence about pole position (DP): 3.49

Interpretations

95 percent confidence level: A.D. 1000-1090
63 percent confidence level: A.D. 1000-1080
Best fit interval: A.D. 1000-1070

Feature 5.1

Provenience: AZ I:10:30, ASM, Feature 5.1 (hearth in Feature 5)
Site Location: T22N R8E Section 33, SW-1/4 NW-1/4 NW-1/4, Zone 12, E449200 N3900900
Magnetic Declination: 10.11 degrees
Latitude: 35.20 degrees
Longitude: 248.37 degrees

Paleomagnetic Results

Alternating field used for demagnetization (EXP): H100 oersteds
Number of samples submitted: 10
Number used for interpretation (N): 10
Mean magnetization (J): 3.45E-03 gauss
Mean paleomagnetic inclination (I): 60.27
Mean paleomagnetic declination (D): 347.66
Radius of 95 percent circle of confidence about mean direction: 2.3
Precision parameter (k): 457.52
Virtual geomagnetic pole latitude (PLAT): 78.54
Virtual geomagnetic pole longitude (PLONG): 193.70
Semimajor axis of 95 percent oval of confidence about pole position (DM): 3.43
Semiminor axis of 95 percent oval of confidence about pole position (DP): 2.60

Interpretations

95 percent confidence level: A.D. 1000-1090, A.D. 1060-1270
63 percent confidence level: A.D. 1030-1090, A.D. 1070-1200
Best fit interval: A.D. 1100-1150

REFERENCES

American Ornithologists' Union
1983 Checklist of North American Birds. 6th edition. Lawrence, Kansas: Allen Press Inc.

Bartlett, Katherine
1934 The material culture of Pueblo II in the San Francisco Mountains, Arizona. Museum of Northern Arizona Bulletin 7. Flagstaff: Museum of Northern Arizona.

1939 A prehistoric "mine" of red argillite resembling pipestone, near Del Rio, Arizona. Museum of Northern Arizona Museum Notes 11(12). Flagstaff: Museum of Northern Arizona.

Bass, William M.
1971 Human Osteology: A Laboratory and Field Manual of the Human Skeleton. Columbia, Missouri: Missouri Archaeological Society, University of Missouri.

Birkby, Walter H.
1973 Discontinuous Morphological Traits of the Skull as Population Markers in the Prehistoric Southwest. MS, doctoral dissertation, Department of Anthropology, University of Arizona, Tucson.

Bohrer, V. L., and K. R. Adams
1977 Ethnobotanical techniques and approaches at Salmon Ruin, New Mexico. Eastern New Mexico University Contributions in Anthropology 8(1). Portales: Eastern New Mexico University.

Breternitz, David A.
1959 Excavations at two Cinder Park phase sites. Plateau 31(3): 66-72.

1966 An appraisal of tree-ring dated pottery of the Southwest. Anthropological Papers of the University of Arizona 10. Tucson: University of Arizona Press.

1967 The eruption(s) of Sunset Crater: Dating and effects. Plateau 40(2): 72-76.

Brothwell, D. B.
1965 Digging Up Bones. London: British Museum of Natural History.

Burt, W. H., and R. Grossenheider
1964 A Field Guide to the Mammals. 2nd edition. Boston: Houghton-Mifflin Company.

1976 A Field Guide to the Mammals. 3rd edition. Boston: Houghton-Mifflin Company.

Castetter, E. F., and W. H. Bell
1942 Pima and Papago Indian Agriculture. Albuquerque: The University of New Mexico Press.

Cockrum, E. Lendell
1960 The Recent Mammals of Arizona: Their Taxonomy and Distribution. Tucson: University of Arizona Press.

1982 Mammals of the Southwest. Tucson: University of Arizona Press.

Colton, Harold S.
1932 Sunset Crater: The effect of a volcanic eruption on an ancient Pueblo people. The Geographical Review 22(4): 582-590.

1937 The eruption of Sunset Crater as an eye witness might have observed it. Museum of Northern Arizona Notes 10(4): 9-12. Flagstaff: Museum of Northern Arizona.

1939 Prehistoric culture units and their relationships in northern Arizona. Museum of Northern Arizona Bulletin 17. Flagstaff: Museum of Northern Arizona.

1941a Winona and Ridge Ruin, Part II. Museum of Northern Arizona Bulletin 19. Flagstaff: Museum of Northern Arizona.

1941b Prehistoric trade in the Southwest. The Scientific Monthly 52: 308-319.

1946 The Sinagua: A summary of the archaeology of the region of Flagstaff, Arizona. Museum of Northern Arizona Bulletin 22. Flagstaff: Museum of Northern Arizona.

1955 Pottery types of the Southwest. Museum of Northern Arizona Ceramic Series 3. Flagstaff: Museum of Northern Arizona.

1956 Pottery types of the Soutwest. Museum of Northern Arizona Ceramic Series 3C. Flagstaff: Museum of Northern Arizona.

1958a Pottery types of the Southwest. Museum of Northern Arizona Ceramic Series 3D. Flagstaff: Museum of Northern Arizona.

1958b Precipitation about the San Francisco Peaks, Arizona. Museum of Northern Arizona Technical Series 2. Flagstaff: Museum of Northern Arizona.

Colton, Harold S., and Lyndon L. Hargrave
1937 Handbook of northern Arizona pottery wares. Museum of Northern Arizona Bulletin 11. Flagstaff: Museum of Northern Arizona.

Cutler, Hugh
1960 Cultivated plant remains from Waterfall Cave, Chihuahua. American Antiquity 26(2): 277-279.

1966 Corn, cucurbits and cotton from Glen Canyon. University of Utah Anthropological Papers 80. Salt Lake City: University of Utah Press.

DeBoer, Warren R.
1980 The prehistoric Sinagua: The view from Mount Elden. USDA Forest Service, Southwestern Region, Cultural Resources Report 34. Albuquerque: U.S. Forest Service.

Di Peso, Charles C.
1956 The upper Pima of San Cayetano del Tumacacori: An archaeohistorical reconstruction of the Ootam of the Pimeria Alta. The Amerind Foundation 7. Dragoon, Arizona: The Amerind Foundation.

Doyel, David E.
1978 The Miami Wash Project: Hohokam and Salado in the Globe-Miami Area, central Arizona. Arizona State Museum Contribution to Highway Salvage Archaeology in Arizona 52. Tucson: University of Arizona.

1979 Archaeological investigations at AZ BB:13:14 in the Tucson Basin, Arizona. Arizona State Museum Contribution to Highway Salvage Archaeology in Arizona 58. Tucson: University of Arizona.

Ferg, Alan
1984 Nonutilitarian groundstone, crystals, and minerals. In "Hohokam Habitation Sites in the Northern Santa Rita Mountains," by Alan Ferg, Kenneth C. Rozen, William L. Deaver, Martyn D. Tagg, David A. Phillips, Jr., and David A. Gregory. Arizona State Museum Archaeological Series 147 (2): 665-699. Tucson: University of Arizona.

Fish, Paul R.
1974 Prehistoric land use in the Perkinsville Valley. The Arizona Archaeologist 8: 1-36. Phoenix: Arizona Archaeological Society.

Fish, Paul R., Peter J. Pilles, Jr., and Suzanne K. Fish
1980 Colonies, traders and traits: The Hohokam in the north. In "Current Issues in Hohokam Prehistory," edited by David Doyel and Fred Plog. Arizona State University Anthropological Research Papers 23: 151-175. Tempe: Arizona State University.

Franklin, Hayward H.
1980 Excavations at Second Canyon Ruin, San Pedro Valley, Arizona. Arizona State Museum Contribution to Highway Salvage Archaeology in Arizona 60. Tucson: University of Arizona.

Fulton, William Shirley
1934a Archaeological notes on Texas Canyon, Arizona. Contributions from the Museum of the American Indian, Heye Foundation 12(1). New York: Museum of the American Indian, Heye Foundation.

1934b Archaeological notes on Texas Canyon, Arizona. Contributions from the Museum of the American Indian, Heye Foundation 12(2). New York: Museum of the American Indian, Heye Foundation.

Galinat, W. C., P. C. Mangelsdorf, and L. Pierson
1956 Estimates of teosinte introgression in archaeological maize. Botanical Museum Leaflets 17(4): 101-124. Cambridge: Harvard University.

Genoves, Santiago
1967 Proportionality of the long bones and their relation to stature among Mesoamericans. American Journal of Physical Anthropology 26(1): 67-77.

Gladwin, Harold S., Emil W. Haury, E. B. Sayles, and N. Gladwin
1937 Excavations at Snaketown: Material Culture. Tucson: University of Arizona Press.

Haas, Jonathan
1971 The Ushlish Ruin, a Preliminary Report of a Colonial Hohokam Period Site in the Lower Tonto Basin, Central Arizona. MS, Arizona State Museum Library, University of Arizona, Tucson.

Hall, Raymond E., and Keith R. Kelson
1959 The Mammals of North America. New York: The Ronald Press Company.

Hantman, Jeffery L, Kent G. Lightfoot, Steadman Upham, Fred Plog, Stephen Plog, and Bruce Donaldson
1984 Cibola Whitewares: A regional perspecitive. In "Regional Analysis of Prehistoric Ceramic Variation: Contemporary Studies of Cibola Whitewares," edited by Alan P. Sullivan and Jeffery L. Hantman. Arizona State University Anthropological Research Papers 31: 17-35. Tempe: Arizona State University.

Haury, Emil W.
1976 The Hohokam: Desert Farmers and Craftsmen. Tucson: University of Arizona Press.

Hoffman, Teresa L., David E. Doyel, and Mark Elson
1983 Ground Stone Tool Production in the New River Basin. Paper presented at the 1983 Hohokam Symposium, Arizona State University, Tempe. MS, Arizona State Museum Library, University of Arizona, Tucson.

Hoffmeister, Donald F., and Steven Carothers
1969 Mammals of Flagstaff, Arizona. Plateau 41(4): 184-188.

Hohman, John W.
1982 Sinagua social differentiation: Inferences based on prehistoric mortuary practices. Arizona Archaeologist 17. Phoenix: Arizona Archaeological Society.

Huckell, Bruce B.
1984 The Archaic occupation of the Rosemont area, Santa Rita Mountains, southeastern Arizona. Arizona State Museum Archaeological Series 147(1). Tucson: University of Arizona.

Hudgens, Bruce R.
1974 Turkey Hills Community: A Sinagua Settlement Pattern Study. MS, Museum of Northern Arizona, Flagstaff.

Jones, Volney H.
1941 Architectural and material culture. In "Winona and Ridge Ruin, Part 1," by John C. McGregor. Museum of Northern Arizona Bulletin 18: 295-299. Flagstaff: Museum of Northern Arizona.

1949 Report on vegetal material. In "Nalakihu: Excavations at a Pueblo III site on Wupatki National Monument, Arizona," by Dale S. King. Museum of Northern Arizona Bulletin 23: 152-157. Flagstaff: Museum of Northern Arizona.

Kaplan, Lawrence
1956 The cultivated beans of the prehistoric Southwest. Annals of the Missouri Botanical Garden 43: 189-251.

Kelly, Isabel T.
1978 The Hodges Ruin: A Hohokam community in the Tucson Basin. Anthropological Papers of the University of Arizona 30. Tucson: University of Arizona Press.

Kelly, Roger E.
1971a Salvage excavations at six Sinagua sites. Plateau 41(3): 112-132.

1971b Diminishing Returns: Twelfth and Thirteenth Century Sinagua Environmental Adaptation in North Central Arizona. MS, doctoral dissertation, Department of Anthropology, University of Arizona, Tucson.

Kent, Kate Peck
1954 Montezuma Castle archeology, Part 2: Textiles. Southwestern Monuments Association Technical Series 3(2). Globe, Arizona: Gila Pueblo.

Kluth, Charles F.
1974 Geology of Mount Elden Area, Coconino County, Arizona. MS, master's thesis, Northern Arizona University, Flagstaff.

Lindsay, Alexander J. Jr., J. Richard Ambler, Mary Anne Stein, and Philip M. Hobler
1968 Survey and excavations north and east of Navajo Mountain, Utah, 1959-1962. Museum of Northern Arizona Bulletin 45. Glen Canyon Series 8. Flagstaff: Museum of Northern Arizona.

Lowe, Charles H.
1980 The Vertebrates of Arizona. Tucson: University of Arizona Press.

Madsen, John
1982 A Sinagua Procurement Strategy: Studies in Least Cost Behavior. MS, masters thesis, Department of Anthropology, California State University, Sacramento.

McGregor, John C.
1936 The culture of sites which were occupied shortly before the eruption of Sunset Crater. Museum of Northern Arizona Bulletin 9. Flagstaff: Museum of Northern Arizona.

1941 Winona and Ridge Ruin, Part I: Architecture and material culture. Museum of Northern Arizona Bulletin 18. Flagstaff: Museum of Northern Arizona.

McGuire, Randall H., and Christian E. Downum
1982 A preliminary consideration of desert-mountain trade relations. In Mogollon Archaeology: Proceedings of the 1980 Mogollon Conference, edited by Patrick H. Beckett and Kira Silverbird, pp. 111-122. Ramona, California: Acoma Books.

Morris, Earl H., and Robert F. Burgh
1954 Basketmaker II sites near Durango, Colorado. Carnegie Institute of Washington Publication 604.

Neily, Robert B.
1983 The Prehistoric Community on the Colorado Plateau: An Approach to the Study of Change and Survival in the Northrn San Juan Area of the American Southwest. MS, doctoral dissertation, Department of Anthropology, Southern Illinois University, Carbondale.

Officer, James E.
1978 Shell. In "The Hodges Ruin: A Hohokam Community in the Tucson Basin," by Isabel T. Kelly. Anthropological Papers of the University of Arizona 30. Tucson: University of Arizona Press.

Pailes, Richard A.
1963 An Analysis of the Fitch Site and its Relation to the Hohokam Classic Period. MS, master's thesis, Arizona State University, Tempe.

Panshin, A. J., and Carl de Zeeuw
1980 Textbook of Wood Technology. New York: McGraw-Hill.

Pilles, Peter J., Jr.
1969 Habitation and field houses near Winona and Angell, Arizona. Kiva 34(2 and 3): 90-102.

1978 The field house and Sinagua demography. In "Limited Activity and Occupation Sites: A Collection of Conference Papers," edited by Albert E. Ward. Contributions to Anthropological Studies 1: 119-133. Albuquerque: Center for Anthropological Studies.

1979 Sunset Crater and the Sinagua: A new interpretation. In Volcanic Activity and Human Activity, edited by Payson D. Sheets and Donald K. Grayson, pp. 459-485. New York: Academic Press.

Reid, J. Jefferson
1984 What is Black-on-white and vague all over? In "Regional Analysis of Prehistoric Ceramic Variation: Contemporary Studies of Cibola Whitewares," edited by Alan P. Sullivan and Jeffery L. Hantman. Arizona State University Anthropological Research Papers 31: 135-152. Tempe: Arizona State University.

Robbins, Chandler S., Bertel Bruin, and Herbert Zim
1966 A Guide to Field Identification of Birds of North America. New York: Golden Press.

Robinson, William J., and Jeffery S. Dean
1969 Tree-ring Evidence for Climatic Changes in the Prehistoric Southwest from A.D. 1000 to 1200. MS, report to the National Park Service from the Laboratory of Tree-Ring Research. Tucson: University of Arizona.

Rondeau, Michael F.
1975 Projectile Point Analysis for the Kahorsho Site: NA 10,937, Central Arizona. MS, master's thesis, Department of Anthropology, California State University, Sacramento.

Rozen, Kenneth C.
1981 Patterned associations among lithic technology, site content, and time: Results of the TEP St. Johns Project lithic analysis. In "Prehistory of the St. Johns Area, East-Central Arizona: The TEP St. Johns Project," by Deborah Westfall. Arizona State Museum Archaeological Series 153: 157-232. Tucson: University of Arizona.

Schour, I., and M. Massler
1941 The developement of the human dentition. Journal of American Dental Association 28: 1153-1160.

Schroeder, Albert H.
1965 Pattern diffusion from Mexico into the Southwest after A.D. 600. American Antiquity 31: 683-704.

Shoemaker, Eugene M.
1977 Eruption History of Sunset Crater, Arizona. Investigator's Annual Report. Wupatki-Sunset Crater National Monument.

Smith, Watson
1952 Excavations in Big Hawk Valley, Wupatki National Monument, Arizona. Museum of Northern Arizona Bulletin 24. Flagstaff: Museum of Northern Arizona.

Stanislawski, Michael B.
1963 Wupatki Pueblo: A Study in Cultural Fusion and Change in Sinagua and Hopi Prehistory. MS, doctoral dissertation, Department of Anthropology, University of Arizona, Tucson.

Stebbins, Robert C.
1966 A Field Guide to Western Reptiles and Amphibians. Boston: Houghton-Mifflin Company.

Sullivan, Alan P.
1980 Arizona Department of Transportation Project F 037-1 (8), Townsend-Divide, Unit 1, U.S. 89, Flagstaff-Cameron Highway, Coconino County, Arizona. MS, Arizona State Museum Library, University of Arizona, Tucson.

1984 Sinagua agricultural strategies and Sunset Crater volcanism. In "Prehistoric Agricultural Strategies in the Southwest," edited by Suzanne K. Fish and Paul R. Fish. Arizona State University Anthropological Research Papers 33: 85-100. Tempe: Arizona State University.

Tagg, Martyn D.
1984a Utilitarian ground stone. In "Hohokam Habitation Sites in the Northern Santa Rita Mountains," by Alan Ferg, Kenneth C. Rozen, William L. Deaver, Martyn D. Tagg, David A. Phillips, and David A. Gregory. Arizona State Museum Archaeological Series 147(2): 605-664. Tucson: University of Arizona.

Tagg, Martyn D.
1984b The Timba-Sha Survey and Boundary Fencing Project, Archeological Investigations at Death Valley National Monument. Western Archeological and Conservation Center Publications in Anthropology 27. Tucson: Western Archeological and Conservation Center, National Park Service.

Tagg, Martyn D., and Bruce B. Huckell
1984 The Sycamore Canyon sites. In "Miscellaneous Archaeological Studies in the ANAMAX-Rosemont Land Exchange Area," by Martyn D. Tagg, Richard G. Ervin, and Bruce B. Huckell. Arizona State Museum Archaeological Series 147 (4): 61-106. Tucson: University of Arizona.

Vokes, Arthur
1983 Shell in the Salt-Gila Aquaduct assemblage. In "Hohokam Archaeology Along the Salt-Gila Aquaduct, Central Arizona Project, Vol. VIII, Material Culture," edited by Lynn S. Teague and Patricia L. Crown. Arizona State Museum Archaeological Series 150(8): 465-550. Tucson: University of Arizona.

Walker, Ernest P.
1975 Mammals of the World. Third edition. Baltimore: John Hopkins University Press.

Whiting, Alfred F.
1966 Ethnobotany of the Hopi. Flagstaff: Northland Press.

Wilson, John P.
1969 The Sinagua and Their Neighbors. MS, doctoral dissertation, Department of Anthropology, Harvard University, Cambridge.

Woodbury, Richard B.
1954 Prehistoric stone implements of northeastern Arizona, reports of the Awatovi Expedition. Papers of the Peabody Museum of American Archaeology and Ethnology 34(6). Cambridge: Harvard University Press.